Born in Courtown Harbour, Dermot O'Neill acquired an early interest in the sea. In 1991 Dermot decided to follow his life-long dream to sail the Atlantic single-handed. The voyage set him on a life-long course in search of spiritual growth. He now lives in Mallorca, Spain.

SEASCAPES
and
ANGELS

Dermot O'Neill

The Collins Press

Published in 2000 by
The Collins Press
West Link Park
Doughcloyne
Wilton
Cork

British Library Cataloguing in Publication data.

Typesetting by The Collins Press Ltd.

Printed in Ireland by Betaprint.

ISBN: 1-898256-86-1

The Threshold

... the point of entering, the outset, the limit of consciousness, the point of beginning, the point at which the stimulus brings a response.

Reference Dictionary

Dermot climbed into bed soon after the moon, his only companion, had slipped from the night sky leaving an emptiness too dark for him to share. There was little to be gained from keeping watch – visibility was poor and he felt a few hours rest was far more important.

Somehow he slept for four adjoining hours and when he woke the wind had eased slightly yet the waves remained big and threatening. Disillusioned with the ocean, he could not be bothered to hoist more sail and wanted to be as far from boat and sea as was possible.

The day passed slowly. He lay outside in the cockpit watching the boat surf on the big rolling seas. Ordinarily the sight of *Poitín's* wake would have aroused excitement and enthusiasm but on this occasion he could not care less. Grey clouds crept across the sky, compounding the sense of isolation and loneliness. He was exhausted by the alien environment and the emotions it evoked. Distance, time, space, no longer offered any meaning. They had chipped away at him over the previous weeks, changing the way he saw himself, crushing him beneath their combined power until he felt he no longer accounted for anything of value on this planet. And now this growing feeling of insignificance, this downward spiral of self-evaluation never before experienced, gave no indication of how low he would go.

It was inconceivable how he had ever convinced himself he was suited to single-handed sailing. The dream, for so long cherished, now seemed like childish folly in the hard reality of an angry ocean. Years of carefully building an ego, of nurturing self-esteem, accounted for nothing. No amount of fancy cars or trendy clothes or cool talking could change the situation in which he had so willingly placed himself. All sense of personal worth was shattered by a cruel environment that regarded his greatest endeavour with contempt – contempt that savaged, ripping away layer after layer of protective self-image to expose a raw and vulnerable soul.

The world in which he once lived continued to exist but he was no longer a part of it. Each family member, each lover and friend could be located in his mind, yet hour upon hour of one-way conversations served only to remind him of the isolation. Somewhere in mid-Atlantic, somewhere between departure and arrival, somewhere within the smallest of specks on the vast expanse of ocean was a world apart which could not be reached. There was no short way out of the solitude he had so naively sought. It was not a game where he could simply call on the radio and ask to be rescued, taken to the safety of the nearest port. The only way out was through more of the same, yet the thought of another day alone, another solitary second, drove an aching through him, through the boat, the sky, the vast empty ocean. He had sailed into a vacuum – through which the grieving and pain of the world must flow before being blessed with joy and returned. The emptiness of a hundred oceans, the pain of a thousand lifetimes, passed through him on their way to keep someone company. This was far worse than he could ever have imagined, far more than he felt capable of coping with and all the while his precious stores of mental endurance were being devoured by blind desperation without any land in sight.

There were times when he had doubted the existence of a God or a power of sorts which controlled his world. Now he felt certain it existed but was oblivious to his plight. He was alone with forces so almighty he could not but question his very existence. The physical danger no longer mattered – it was the feeling of nothingness which weighed so heavily on what remained of his shattered soul that threatened to destroy him.

He had wanted to go to the edge of excitement and fear to see how he would survive and, with the help of a little solitude, explore his soul. Feeling mentally low was to be expected but depression was new and frightening. Never had he given serious consideration to the prospect of reaching his emotional limit and now that it had started there was nothing he could do to halt the slide; deeper and deeper, into the blackest of depression, depression which ruthlessly dragged him towards the brink of blind despair.

Hour after hour, maybe days, he fought the demon of despair and the abyss from where it came. Heaving like a man possessed, an emotional vomit, retching, clearing the bile from the depths of heart and mind, he clawed his way back from the hole that awaited.

Without the daily audience to perform to there was no longer any ego. Without crew, he was safe from stories which might be carried home to contemporaries. For the first time in his adult life he was free – free to express himself as he so wished without apologies to anyone. Alone he cried – huddled in the cockpit, physically sick, sore from days of stomach cramp, mentally exhausted from lack of sleep. He cried because he could do so without manly shame; because he was reminded of childhood when tears were shed for the sake of it; because he once accepted that big boys don't cry.

In the face of such honesty all adult barriers seemed juvenile in the solitude of the ocean. His mind escaped into early childhood years and he experienced the joy of being a seven-year old once again. The loving, uncomplicated child was vulnerable in his desire for love and affection and had not yet acquired the defences necessary to protect against the hurtful jibes society had to offer. For years he believed he had grown up and become an adult but alone on the ocean, he realised the adult was also the boy. Like a Russian doll with every stage of life to date contained within the next, he saw a core soul dressed in life's experiences. The past with today added. A child in adult's skin.

As a man he had endeavoured to put the past behind and get on with living but he now saw it was a living thing, feeding the present with filtered thoughts and emotions. The childhood memories associated with the good times remained in his mind, as did confusion and shame, but he could now reassess it with the knowledge of an adult.

Feeling stronger for the hours of tears he slowly crawled onto the cabin floor. Numb – drained of every emotion he ever knew. A savaged and mutilated soul. Emotional remains laid to rest somewhere in mid-Atlantic. He slept well, like a babe, oblivious to the violent motion of the boat or the madness that raged outside.

***

Dermot was awake long before his mind told him so – long before the slightest suggestion that he should get up on deck, check for shipping and adjust the sails. A blessed period of time in which to feel the wounds of yesterday knit together and heal. Wounds which might mature into scars if ignored. He bathed in a feeling of gentle emotions, his mind having the decency to hold its tongue.

Eventually he found the strength to venture outside. The elements welcomed him with the enthusiasm of a successful midwife; a painful birth and the customary crack on the arse to induce the first tears of life being over. He wedged into the corner of the cockpit and enjoyed the brown-rich smell of breakfast coffee. Between clouds an immature sun, low in the sky, threw long lazy smiles upon his face. Reflections bounced across the rippled swells like giggles between the smiles and landed on board, setting the air alight. Warm and safe, he snuggled in *Poitín*'s lap and allowed a growing feeling of kindness to occupy his heart. As always his mind interrupted, questioning feelings.

Confronted by this relentless chatter, his feelings were easily defeated in such a debate. But exhausted from yesterday's showdown, his mind soon ran out of puff and left him again to the quiet of his heart. Thankfully, feelings returned and grew. Kindness matured into love and for once was reflected on himself. His own adult emotions, so often rationed to starving lovers for fear of reciprocation, poured into his day. The sails tingled with swollen delight and carried him over new ground. His mind attempted to interrupt once more but was overcome.

The morning breeze grew thick with love and fun and freedom. Something touched him like never before. The endless horizon came into view and the sweetest of young air flowed across his palate, its freshness clearing his mind. His senses indulged in this unexpected feast and a silent whisper reassured that he was not alone. The vacuum through which he had sailed now gushed with gentleness and caring – the healing had begun now the poison was removed.

Time only exists when asked. An exhausted mind, unable to ask, left him to enjoy a day-long moment. Engulfed by perfection, he was suspended in time.

All is directed at him, he is the centre of attention. For the very first time he feels the presence of absolute power. A power capable of crushing anything that chooses to threaten its existence. Earlier feelings of insignificance are now placed into perspective, the physical. A new-found sense of love opens a belief in himself and the knowledge that his soul is of absolute importance to this

Power. Suspended in the most blissful of states he now knows he will never be alone. Threadbare doubts about a God, a Supernatural, are already discarded. There can be no turning back now he has seen his true physical insignificance, his real spiritual importance. This was not what he expected to find in mid-Atlantic but neither is he surprised. The real surprise will surface in future months as each second of this experience unfolds, teaching whatever he needs to know – stars by which to navigate his life.

Cradled and nursed back to full strength by the mother of all mothers, healing the wounds from the day before, he is carried to bed. Sleepy eyes – looking at the night sky, he curls into the foetal position and sleeps like a cradled child. Sleepy head – images flooding through his mind, he dreams a dream:

A sea of dreams lapping on a shore. Slowly he walks through moon-lit water. Ripples obscure the bottom, a path through the flooded rocks. Where he stands, a beautiful world of colour and shapes appears. A world shimmering through a liquid crystal. Shells stuffed with dreams, ready to feed his soul. Where to begin, he glances from mussel to clam to periwinkle; each one full and lush. He ponders a clam and waits for a dream to unfold. The night passes, moving from shell to shell, dream upon dream, some clear and vivid, others needing time to digest.

Dusk quietly arrives to clear away the night sky and lay the table for day. He reaches down to gather his catch but finds they are not where they appear, forever safe in the liquid crystal.

Time demands attention and hurries everything along. The sun dutifully raises its head from the depths of the sea, water rushes in to fill the void. He looks with anticipation as the liquid thins. Shells full of dreams, about to become real, slowly close to protect against the sharp light of day.

In the morning he lay in bed picking through the memory; beach-combing for mussels, periwinkles and clams. Sensing how dreams feed the soul and that much is lost to the sharp scrutiny of the mind, he abandoned the search.

A Greater Work of Art

Dermot had breakfast with his parents on the morning of departure, and was reminded of his first day at school; everyone avoiding the unsavoury event which lay ahead.

His father Tom, almost five years retired, quizzed him about pension funds, the stock market and interest rates. Dermot's all too familiar answers helped pass the time, demanded nothing of his brain but served as a reminder that he had turned his back on a good accountancy career – an unacceptable sin in the eyes of his father for which the awkward penance was regularly extracted; a fiscal inquisition of one who might have ascended through the hierarchy of commerce but for lack of conviction. How anyone could refuse such a golden opportunity was beyond his father but he saw it more as a silver spoon rammed into his gob at the first mention of a career in Marine Biology.

Sam the dog, sensing the friction, decided to take up his usual vantage point in front of the Aga stove, his bloated bulk flopping on the floor as he prepared to absorb the heat of the cast-iron into his arthritic back. To most people, the name Sam seemed totally inadequate for a five-stone shaggy sheepdog of exceptional character, thus the need to qualify his name at each mention. He was a superb creature in his prime, before being neutered to help curb his wanderings. Now he was seeing out his days just being fat, comfortable and very obedient. Dermot failed to recognise the lesson Sam the professor had to offer.

Marie made an art form of pottering around her kitchen, ensuring there was always a boiling kettle on tea duty, a fruit bowl in season and a fridge bursting with home cooking on permanent standby. She never knew when her eldest son might visit but when he did there was no doubt as to his destination once the 'hello's were said. The thought of not seeing the familiar sight of Dermot's rear sticking out of the refrigerator as he searched for goodies gripped her heart.

She removed the jabbering frying pan from the stove and side-stepped Sam the hog. Her own arthritic body winced at the discomfort she could inflict by asking the old mutt to move, for it seemed they were comrades in pain. She forced her attention to focus on preparing the last great Irish breakfast her boy would eat for over a year. What he would eat, or when or how, were things she could not bring herself to consider without tears of despair welling up inside. How he would survive the Atlantic Ocean alone terrified her but she was determined to see her son off with a full belly and the fullest of support. Tears would not be shed lightly for fear of weakening his resolve.

Marie prided herself on offering variety rather than quantity when cooking. All he had asked for was fried egg and bacon but what was lovingly placed in front of him were fried eggs, white pudding, black pudding, sausage and a little smoked bacon for good measure. The sheer variety disguised the vast amount of food, far more than he dare eat. Pausing for a moment, he savoured the still life plated before his eyes and the portrait of a proud mother who hoped that one breakfast would give her son the strength needed for the entire Atlantic voyage.

Before the activity surrounding breakfast had time to settle, he was up and about, checking bags, passport, boat's papers – anything to distract their frightened minds.

***

The time finally came to cast off. The tide was about to turn and the boat ready to go. The sound of the tiny diesel engine skimmed across the smooth surface of the river, bounced off the quay walls and rushed back to identify *Poitín* as the scoundrel. He stepped ashore and hugged his Mum, a long loving hug, and simply told her to look after herself. Her earlier dry-eyed support gave way to tears of confusion. The mighty Marie O'Neill, the rearer of children, the climber of mountains, his loving mother, stood shattered by the fear of what might be. If she only knew how she had helped to sow the seed of this crazy dream, a dream that was about to place her son's life in the fate of the gods.

He turned to his Dad. At first they shook hands but then hugged and wished each other well. There was an awkward silence and for a moment it seemed they had something more to say. They both hesitated, but still there was nothing, and the opportunity passed when years of silent frustration might at least have been acknowledged. Feeling awkward yet relieved, they smiled and said goodbye.

Dermot stepped onto the boat, calculating each step, pacing each movement as if walking on ice. He was desperate to conceal the welling emotions which he feared might crack the surface calm. Time lapsed between action and awareness, leaving him seconds behind. Somehow the lines were untied and *Poitín* drifted away from the concrete jetty. His parents stood looking confused and miserable as the boat departed. They waved from the shore like flags at half-mast and his heart ached for the pain which only he inflicted. They feared for their son's life and would continue to worry every minute of every day until his return. This he knew, but it could not be avoided unless he was to live life just to please them. They had questioned why he was attempting such a crazy thing, yet he sensed they appreciated the need.

Well-rehearsed determination helped carry the moment. 'I'll write and phone,' he shouted, the words blunted by a dry nervous mouth. 'Don't worry, *Poitín* will take care of me. You look after yourselves.'

While his stomach churned with anxiety, his head throbbed with blind excitement. Slowly he edged towards his first ocean crossing, alone. At last he had finally done it, he had taken the first step. It didn't really matter how far he sailed. He was happy knowing a chance had been taken in life not to benefit pocket or ego but to explore his soul. 'Maybe I'll make it across the ocean, maybe I won't,' he thought, knowing his Creator could hear. 'But at least I tried.' This was surely the most exciting of life's adventures. 'Yeeee haaaaa!' he snarled.

Tom paced *Poitín* from the quay, calling anxiously, 'Dermot, the eh ... the dinghy seems to be loose at this side. See ... there,' pointing to a line which might threaten his son's safety.

Dermot was infuriated by what he saw as yet more ridicule from someone he could never please and lashed out with a sharp reply. No sooner were the words spoken than the situation had to be recovered. 'I can't leave like this,' he thought, 'why couldn't he just let it go, I can do this without his interference.'

'Sorry,' he shouted without feeling regret. 'I'll fix it in a minute.'

The river pushed towards the ebbing tide that waited to pull him seaward; combined strength from an unseen friend to help overcome a most fragile moment. A special companion who willed him on his way and would be there in the months ahead to save him from himself.

***

For Dermot, that anxious morning appeared to be the first step of an exceptional adventure and a new soul-searching experience. Had he the knowledge at the time to look a little deeper he would have recognised a chain of events linking each step of a journey that began long before he really appreciated his soul.

Many years previously, when frustrated with an accountancy career in Dublin and demented by a young appetite for life, he decided to try the other side of the world for excitement. His sister had lived in Sydney and by her accounts it offered the perfect lifestyle for a 25 year-old 'boyo' who loved outdoor life.

Dermot spent four great years in Australia, most of it in Sydney with the exception of a few month's holidays exploring the vastness of that exciting continent. Life in Sydney kicked off to a cracking start. He landed a superb job and suddenly found himself with plenty of spare cash. It wasn't long before he had acquired a cool apartment by the water and a fancy car in which to transport his ego. Life was good, simple and lots of fun. After a sluggish start with the local females he found himself on a roll. Girls looking for fun were not left wanting, while those in search of something deeper were courted to the brink of love, only to be abandoned out of fear.

He used what attributes he possessed to the full and made sure to compensate for his failings. A boyish mischievousness endeared him to his male friends and prevented them from taking him too seriously. Some women found it refreshing, in a naive sort of way. A sense of humour concealed his shyness to such an extent that only the closest of friends saw the vulnerability he struggled to protect. They could sense an inner strength but were sometimes left dumbfounded by his displays of insecurity in certain social situations.

In moments spent alone, away from the distraction of contemporaries, his true self surfaced, hinting at a sense of purpose in life. What this purpose was or when it would be uncovered were beyond his conscious mind. It was the subliminal taunting that his day awaited which saved him from self-destruction.

Regardless of how he indulged in the good times there was always the inkling that life had something greater to offer. It was a strange combination of inkling and ego which prompted him to acquire his first sailing boat. The ego was quickly satisfied by day trips within the safety of the harbour, but as the party goers fell by the wayside he began sailing further afield and alone. His childhood dream of crossing the Atlantic single-handed, 'just like the great Sir Francis Chichester' began peeking through the maze of his adult aspirations.

Of all the experiences 'down under' it was an evening spent at a reception in the Sydney Opera House which really tickled him. Standing outside on the upper balcony he was touched by the power of that unique theatre, with its porcelain semi-domes which peaked overhead as demi-gods to art and architecture. He took time to savour the newness of this exciting place. A galaxy of lights arched the Harbour Bridge and defined the city night. Ferries hustled back and forth from Circular Quay like comets across the reflected sky. The balmy night air, alien to Celtic skin, confirmed a foreign land.

Dermot felt elevated in his own estimation, a sculptor of life serving his time to the trade. He had created his first major work, the 'City of Sydney', dripping in the splendour of its famous jewels, waiting patiently for the aspiring master to dare wish. He raised his champagne, the winners bouquet, and asked to discover his greatness. Nothing more. How was he to know that his greatest moment lay a decade away in mid-Atlantic. He had wished for an awakening which would last a lifetime, something for which he was not yet prepared.

Near the end of his third year in Sydney he realised he might not always have the opportunity to achieve the youthful dream of sailing an ocean alone. Like most young people he was complacent about time, assuming there was an endless supply of years in which to live life. That belief was shattered late one winter's night as he lay drunk on the sitting-room floor, surrounded by the shrapnel of yet another bash, a minefield of beer cans, fast food cartons and ashtrays. Deep in the back of his mind, above the high pitched whine of an empty TV screen, the phone rang.

His brother sounded confused at first, then apologised for the hurt he was about to deliver; the first girl Dermot had truly loved was dead, killed in a car crash.

Dermot's mind went blank; the process of self-preservation

12

in which a heart seeks to protect itself. Slowly, very slowly, snippets of related sentences began to trickle through his mind – sufficient detail to conduct a conversation but never so much to seek the sense in such a waste of life. Andriena and he had loved to the full, the youngest and most passionate of loves. Like juvenile buds they had unfolded into individual flowers and discovered life together. It seemed their summer would never end. But in time it was the strong wills and craving for life which had first drawn them together that drove them down separate roads. Parting was a long and painful process. Chance meetings became opportunities which grew increasingly frequent but each night served to confirm the sad realisation that they would eventually destroy each other. Love gave them the strength to finally part and left a place in their hearts for the sweetest of memories.

A chapter in his life which could never be reopened stirred deep regrets. She was so full of fun, it seemed her death was a dreadful mistake and that God had got it very wrong. He could not understand how someone who had so much to offer this world was no longer allowed to participate. He was gripped by the realisation that any dreams she may have had would remain unfulfilled and that contrary to what people say, life does not go on – for some it stops all too soon. It would take many years of learning before such apparent vandalism by the gods could be viewed as a brush stroke on a greater work of art.

Andriena's tragic death shocked Dermot into looking at his own life, at life in general and the role in which he was cast. He needed to look within and find the truth. Australia had helped him along the waiting road but he needed to slow down. The time seemed right to return to his roots.

***

Dermot left a good accountancy position in Sydney to return to Ireland and take over the family hotel. His parents had built a thriving business during the previous 25 years but in recent times they had lost trade to younger, more enthusiastic opposition. It appeared to be an ideal opportunity and with plenty of hard work and imagination, he felt that within three to four years, he could turn the business around. His parents accepted he would eventually sell the hotel but they had hoped that by then he would at last be ready to settle down.

It took little time to re-establish himself in his home town of Arklow, County Wicklow, an old seafaring port well accustomed to the comings and goings of men for long periods at a time. 'The last stronghold of sail', as it had been so lovingly christened many years ago, was a town crewed by a proud people who in a changing world had so doggedly refused to turn their backs on their beloved sailing ships. Age-old skills, tempered to a razor's edge, had passed from father to son; the sharpness of an eye capable of squeezing an extra knot from the sails of a proud old schooner, the gentle touch from a powerful hand well accustomed to nudging a mighty craft into port on the hint of a breeze, the sensitivity of a weather-beaten nose that sniffed the horizon for the safest passage home.

But the finest and the fastest of sailing schooners first put to the test by steam were eventually rendered obsolete by the diesel engine. Fleet upon fleet was savaged by the new form of power which miraculously stole the wind from their canvas. Sails once admired for their ingenuity and power became an obstacle to the impatient propeller. Stripped of their foliage, masts were felled, bowsprits hacked off and the naked hulls hauled to the breaker's yard.

Widowed by the passing of their beautiful schooners, old seafarers came home to grieve, while younger men remarried a new generation. Sailors became Merchant Seamen and continued to roam the world but they still longed for the feeling of stability which the familiarity of a home port invoked. If, upon return, their family was where they dropped anchor, it was the local pub where they cleared customs and discharged their cargo of happenings and events.

Dermot had the advantage of being reasonably well known. He made some interesting changes to the hotel – more of a refit than refurbishing, for he viewed the old place as being 'moored' rather then located beside the harbour. Local historians helped him uncover the names of previous proprietors dating back to the 1800s. To his delight one was a ship owner, of sorts – the wife of a schooner captain in fact, but it was enough to establish a seafaring genealogy for the hotel – certainly more than enough to justify the collecting of maritime memorabilia and the mounting of old photos on the walls. He hosted historical lectures which were a huge success and the local press was eventually swept along in his enthusiasm. He aligned himself firmly with the sea and loved every minute of it.

The hotel, once marinated, was rewarded by the patronage of all those who lived or played on the sea. He worked hard, leaving no part of his success to chance but this did not prevent him from burning the candle at the other end. Once again life for Dermot was good, simple and lots of fun. He acquired a sailing boat with which to explore the local coast and with every outing moved closer to his childhood dream, helping it to mature into an adult aspiration. He began to believe that his emotional development was somehow intertwined with the physical and mental challenge of an ocean crossing alone, a goal necessary to fulfil his life.

With the success of the business came the danger of being wedged into a lifetime offering more of the same. With each passing year the fear of change and the need to hold on tighter grew, strangling the very spirit which offered the strength to encompass new horizons.

He was haunted by an image of himself as an old frustrated man looking back over life and thinking, 'why didn't I take a chance when I was young enough'. He promised that would never happen but as he matured and surrounded himself with worldly comforts, the readiness to take chances grew weaker.

To sail an ocean single-handed had always depended on him having sufficient funds to afford a suitable boat. That excuse no longer applied. He had owned *Poitín* for two years and knew how to sail her without crew. The truth was that he had turned 35 and was losing his sense of adventure and belief in youthful dreams. He wondered if he was at last growing up or just growing afraid.

It was Andriena's death which had forced him to question the purpose of life but it was a back injury which prompted him into deciding to do something about it. Soon after he returned from Australia he fell and hurt his back, nothing serious at the time but enough to slow him down for a while.

A few years later the problem returned in the form of two slipped discs and he suddenly found himself without the healthy body he had taken for granted. His nights were sometimes spent on the bedroom floor in search of relief from the spinal throbbing. A doctor treated him on a number of occasions but the relief was always short-lived. Walking or standing for more than an hour used to guarantee severe pain, which was only marginally relieved by a session of manipulative exercises. Eventually he was advised to consider surgery, which he rejected, feeling certain it would weaken his back and leave him physically restricted for the rest of his life.

He would lie in bed at night and wonder if his fears of old age, ill health and a lost dream had become young age, ill health and a lost dream. Had he left it too late and was now being punished by his spirit? He vowed that should he ever return to full health he would undertake the sailing trip. This vow was made with the clearest of minds, centred in the moment through pain – pain which swamped any vision of the future, promising to make it a living hell. Unable to flee to another time he was firmly anchored in the present alongside his true needs and aspirations. There was no escape.

Having read about some people's ability to cure themselves he had a strong belief in the power of the mind over the body.

16

One night when sleeping on the floor he lay on his side, placed a finger on the slipped disc and tried to imagine the flow of energy in his body. As he drifted off to sleep he became aware of his finger pressing firmly against the disc although his arm was totally relaxed. Gradually, the pain was replaced by a feeling of comfort and warmth. For the first time in months, his body relaxed and drifted into a long-awaited sleep.

The following morning he was surprised to find he was free of pain and as the days passed he grew to accept that he had somehow healed himself – quite an amazing experience and one which he tried to repeat on the other disc in his neck but to no avail. It seemed his success at self-healing was due more to beginner's luck than any new-found skill but the experience cemented his belief in the power of the mind. An osteopath manipulated the other slipped disc in his neck and it was not long before he returned to full health.

Once the physical problem was out of the way he was faced with the reality of fulfilling the promise he had so passionately made.

He had spent the previous four years building up a good trade in the hotel. Was he now just going to 'throw' it all away? Selling a successful business in the middle of a recession made absolutely no sense to his parents, his friends or his customers. It would have been acceptable if he intended investing in a bigger and better business but to sell everything to go sailing was another matter. 'You're a gobshite,' declared a friend. 'You're selling this gold mine to frig off in that little boat. What will you do when you get back?'

Dermot struggled for the strength to tell the truth but failed. How could he declare that he was going soul-searching and the sailing was just part of the experience? This weakness taunted his belief in the ability to survive a single-handed ocean crossing. The demons of insecurity reared their heads, comparing him with contemporaries: stable members of society, married with kids and steady jobs. Demons of the mind which soon had him feeling naive and immature.

Moving closer to a decision brought him closer to a point of no return. There was no way he could sell the hotel, do the trip and still have the safety and security of a business waiting when he returned. Once the business and his livelihood were gone he had to set sail, there was no question about that. He had to make a gigantic leap, without room for any half-hearted attempt. Giving up something in which he had invested so much time and effort, something that represented his creativity and business acumen, was an agonising decision.

For months the battle of the 'what if's continued to nag. Every night he lay in bed and wondered if he was doing the right thing. What if the day came to untie *Poitín* and sail away and he hadn't got the stomach for it. He had read of people who had cast off all ties with normal life in pursuit of a dream and found they were just dreamers – people who had pursued a dream to the starting post only to discover they were not capable of seeing it through.

There was a vague picture in his mind of the mental and physical steps that had to be taken to break all ties with everyday life and embark on the voyage. He found the more committed he became to the whole idea of the voyage the more confident he was of himself and the need to pursue it. There was an overwhelming feeling of *déjà vu* – either he had travelled the same path before or had imagined it so often that it now felt familiar.

The first major steps were in motion. An irrevocable promise to set sail had been made and the decision to sell the business was by now a foregone conclusion. All that remained was action.

One particular night he lay awake in bed, staring into the darkness and struggling with the 'what if's about the sale of the business. He decided to stop bombarding himself with questions and listen for a change. As he lay in the stillness of the night the quiet of his mind was broken by the strongest of thoughts telling him what to do. He looked around the room surprised by the clarity of the inner voice and unsure for a moment if it had actually come from within. That voice simply said 'trust yourself'.

It was a vote of confidence in himself and the ability to know what was best. Having taken the time to relax and listen he was rewarded with the very answer he sought. Instinct invariably told him when something was right but was not always heeded. It was obvious what he wanted – he just found it hard to believe that he could be right and everyone else was wrong.

Had he not listened to the inner voice directing him, he would have lived a frustrated life. To live such a life knowing he had turned his back on his potential would have guaranteed a tormented soul and a life of self-destruction. In time he would see that a desire such as this, to express oneself in some way, is a beautiful gift, something to be cherished and explored. Fortunately not everyone is tormented by such desire but those who are must respond or face the consequences. Far too often the fear of the unknown smothers the need for self-expression.

He woke the following morning feeling determined to do what was right. A quick phone call to a local real estate agent put the hotel on the market. Two months later the business was sold and he was free to pursue his dream. He was amazed by the speed at which events moved, as though those same events were waiting to be spurred into action by his very thoughts. The strangest of coincidences slotted into place, one after the other. The slipped disc had surfaced as the business peaked and remained until his decision to set sail. In a market of desperate sellers, potential buyers appeared, with ready funds, seeking a business such as his. Never in the most optimistic of moments could he have expected to sell the hotel with such ease. His intuition, that inner voice, to 'trust yourself' would seek due recognition when the time was right. It seemed his destiny, like a dammed river, breached, flooded towards the future with unstoppable power.

B-R-E-A-D

The final details involving the sale of the hotel were completed by early February, leaving four months in which to prepare for the voyage; far too much time in which to fight off the nagging doubts that sought moments of insecurity. However, there was no other choice but to wait for winter to pass. The decision to sell the business and commit himself to the dream had lifted an enormous weight from his shoulders. Years of imagining, months of dithering, were at last over. Once the plunge had been taken he found himself carried steadily towards the sea by a flow of events and preparations, whose momentum was of his own making.

From this new position of increasing confidence and belief, he was amazed as to how he had contrived for so long to avoid making a decision. Yet when viewed through the eyes of retrospect he could see how life might so easily have persuaded him to do otherwise. Either way there was no going back and he threw himself headlong into preparing the boat.

Poitín was safely nestled in the marina in Kinsale, 150 miles from Arklow. He had cruised the south coast during the summer and decided to leave her there in the hope of fitting in some winter sailing. Kinsale was the safest of 'hidey-holes' along the Fastnet Coast, tucked well away from the Atlantic gales. The old stone harbour which occupied the centre of the town was originally built to facilitate trading vessels. The harbour outlived the trade and then slipped into a long hibernation. Businesses closed, young people emigrated and Kinsale scraped out a living from a few fishing boats and the surrounding farms. Blessed to have escaped the enthusiastic planners of the 1960s the town arrived virtually unscathed into an era of 'old is beautiful'. Gracious old houses were restored rather than modernised, decorative shop fronts were treated to a little make-up rather than a double glazing facelift, and the harbour awakened from its slumber.

A marina was floated into place and moored at the mouth of the old harbour, just far enough back from the river which flowed past the town. After many years the marina still looked new but it appeared to have befriended its stone mentor and quietly went about its business. The fact that the yacht club was wedged in among the local buildings helped greatly with what might have been a difficult upbringing. The old Georgian house was only too aware of its adjoining neighbours and chaperoned its floating prodigy from the quayside. Dermot felt somewhat sorry for the marina, for it seemed that every house in town kept an eye on the newcomer – terrace upon terrace, old upon older, peeking their heads above their more senior residents to ensure that below, all remained well.

Dermot had owned *Poitín* for three years and found her to be a beautiful boat to sail. Although built from fibreglass she had the slender lines of a wooden boat, which pleased him greatly. He heard it said that 'pretty boats sail well', and from the moment he laid eyes on her it was obvious she was seakindly. The teak toe rail and rubbing strake which ran the full length of the hull accentuated her comely contours, as can seamed stockings compliment great legs.

Poitín's conservative shape above deck was pretty to behold and aged her nicely. The combination of cream-coloured deck and coach roof, set against a white hull and blue canvas dodgers could not have been bettered. The modern trend towards all white, flat-decked boats did not sit easy with him. A boat not only had to sail well but needed to blend with the sea and wind like a playful dolphin or swooping bird. A true sailing romantic, he was easily courted by *Poitín*, who in time would expect to be danced across an ocean.

The name *Poitín*, pronounced 'potch-een', also helped to endear her to him as it was taken from the Irish for an illegal moonshine distilled in the more isolated parts of Ireland. A small pot was originally used to collect each sacred drip of alcohol which resulted from a mound of potatoes. And so it was the small pot rather than the sacrificial spuds which claimed the right to name the consummate fire-water. Invariably the illegal purchase was made more from a desire to be mischievous than any liking for raw alcohol. The rogue name gave *Poitín* extra character and set her apart from the likes of *Fast Buck*, *Lazy Days*, or ...

At 28 feet she was considered small for ocean sailing, dangerously small according to some people. Yet she was the biggest boat he had ever sailed, a full-grown ocean yacht in his mind. At first she felt enormous, intimidating almost for someone schooled in dinghies and day-sailers, but it wasn't long before they grew into each other. Over the previous three years she had proven herself in diverse situations and he had grown to appreciate that she was the boat to suit his needs. Nevertheless she was fourteen years old and he needed to look seriously at her structural capacity to undergo a 12,000 mile ocean passage.

He planned to depart Ireland at the beginning of the summer and take advantage of the good weather to cruise the west coast of Europe – maybe even stick his nose round the Rock of Gibraltar and into the Mediterranean. It was important to be well south before the North Atlantic gales set in for the winter. He then hoped to spend time in the Canary Islands and leave for the West Indies in early December, well after the hurricane season had ended. Ideally he could expect reasonable weather but it could not be relied upon. He therefore prepared for the worst because all that was required was one simple mishap to start a chain of events that so often precedes the loss of a boat at sea.

He intended lifting *Poitín* out of the water for a thorough inspection when she returned to Arklow. In the meantime the preparations in Kinsale were confined to those items above the waterline. He began with the basics of sails, engine and electrical system. *Poitín* required a selection of sails which were big enough to sail well in light winds yet sufficiently small to cope in very strong winds. By reducing the sail area in gale conditions he could ensure a more comfortable ride yet maintain enough speed to control the boat.

Unlike some traditionalists who believed an engine to be a luxury in a sailing boat, he regarded it as a critical piece of safety equipment. In situations of little or no wind, where there was a danger of being carried onto rocks by the tide or run down by a ship, an engine was of the utmost importance. The engine also served to generate power, not only for the navigational lights but for other electrical equipment on board such as the VHF radio, which was critical to the overall safety of the boat. Consequently the little twelve horse-power engine was lifted from *Poitín*'s bilge and sent ashore for a complete overhaul.

Never having sailed an ocean before meant he was heading into an unknown, and the prospect of seeing himself react to the challenge of a beautiful yet dangerous environment, when freed from the distractions of everyday life, aroused excitement and fear. There were nights in the marina, with *Poitín* safely tied up, when he listened to the howling wind and tried to imagine her being hammered by an Atlantic gale.

In an attempt to gain some insight into what four or five weeks of solitude might offer, he shut himself on board and vowed to remain in the confines of the cabin for 48 hours. The day began well, listening to the rain on deck and drinking coffee. But then the hours began to drag and he struggled with the day; reading, coffee, writing, tea, reading, cooking, reading, coffee, nibbles, frustration, anxiety ... madness.

Frantic to be off the boat, he scrambled ashore, desperate to make human contact. 'Holy shit!' he thought. 'The great ocean yachtsman has just endured the mighty total of twelve hours, single-handed, in the marina in Kinsale.' It was time for company, indeed time for a busy pub.

The following day offered a bitch of a hangover. Sprinting through his drinks had never been his strong point, especially when a whiskey awaited him at the finish line. His flirtation with solitude had been rewarded with a kiss of madness that sent warning bells ringing through his plans.

Dermot recovered the situation by rationalising that had he simply wanted solitude he could have camped on the side of a mountain for a few months. If he had wanted sailing he could have crewed on a 'round the world' yacht. So why was he doing it? Most of his contemporaries enjoyed racing or cruising in local waters and only ever chanced to read about ocean sailing. What made him think he was any different, when in fact he had less experience than most? For an experienced solo yachtsman to depart on an ocean voyage would not be regarded as a major event, but for someone like Dermot, who was a novice to ocean sailing, to attempt his first Atlantic crossing in a 28-foot yacht was a cause for serious reflection. 'Why do I believe I am capable of something slightly outside the ordinary?' he thought. 'What is it that makes me want to push myself, to stand on top of my mental and physical cliff with my toes out over the edge and see if I can keep my balance?'

Lurking below the physical challenge and the boyhood dream was something buried deep within that needed to be exhumed before it suffocated and was lost forever. Severe action was needed to break through the frozen surface.

The winter passed slowly and he spread the work on *Poitín* to mid-April until ready to sail her back to Arklow. Eager to get going and with the help of a few friends, *Poitín* left Kinsale on a two-day trip to her home port. He was exhilarated by the sail and somehow felt she too enjoyed the little canter along the south coast of Ireland. Feeling her come alive once again aroused emotions for boat and sea. The dream was revitalised and he felt certain that selling the business and committing himself to the trip was the best decision he had ever made.

Now that his taste for sailing was renewed there was no holding back. Bursting with renewed enthusiasm he set about completing the work on *Poitín*. She was lifted out of the water at the local sailing club where he could make a final inspection and paint her with anti-foul.

While making the necessary preparations for *Poitín* and himself, he tried to imagine the worst situations that could be encountered. Having devoured innumerable sailing books and magazines over the years he knew that the biggest disaster that could happen at sea was for a yacht to break up in severe weather conditions. It was more common with old wooden boats but it had been known to happen to fibreglass. Either the boat was badly designed, was too lightly constructed or she had previously suffered damage which was not apparent. When preparing the boat he began by concentrating on the critical area of hull and deck; that they were both firmly joined together and in good condition. Gaining access to each of the 80 bolts which held the deck to the hull involved stripping away part of the interior fittings and crawling into the most inaccessible corners.

He arranged for a professional boat builder from the local yard to check the hull both inside and out and to examine bolts which held the keel in place. There was always the possibility of corrosion or of bolts loosening which would probably cause a leak sufficiently large to sink the boat. Only ten months previously, a boat racing off the south coast of Ireland lost her keel and immediatly capsized. The crew were fortunate enough to be trapped in a pocket of air in the upturned hull where they survived until being rescued.

Another critical situation he needed to consider was the possibility of *Poitín* colliding with something which might puncture the hull. The chances were that a boat travelling at five or six knots would burst open and sink within minutes of hitting a semi-submerged tree trunk or ship's container. There was estimated to be at least 1,000 steel containers floating in the world's oceans-at any one time. A boat manned with a crew of three or four in such a situation could hope to attend to the damaged hull while others manned the pumps and handled the sails. He considered the chances of hitting something to be fairly remote and there was little he could do other than install an electric bilge pump and pray it didn't happen.

The other main areas of concern were the rigging and steering. The prospect of a broken mast or rudder could usually be overcome by jury-rigging some form of emergency system which would see the boat to the nearest port. Fortunately the number of yachts lost each year as a result of these particular breakages was quite small. Yet he inspected every inch of the mast, searching for any signs of fatigue or damage, and replaced all the rigging with heavier wire than was recommended by the manufacturers.

For some reason he appeared to be unreasonably concerned about the steering, that it was strong enough to do the job properly. When inspecting the rudder, he noticed a small crack in the fibreglass casing and leaving nothing to chance, removed it for repair by a specialist boatyard in Dublin. He was relieved to have spotted the problem as the prospect of a broken rudder sent cold, terrifying shivers down his spine. When re-mounting the repaired rudder an inner voice whispered that all was not well but he dismissed it as jitters; an adult response to the notion that anything other than hard fact should be heeded smothered intuition, long since consigned to the same fate as fairy stories.

He sought the help and advice of a few select people, but to most he declared he was simply taking *Poitín* on a sail to Gibraltar. This lie he justified as not wanting to worry his parents unnecessarily but the truth was he still feared the possibility that

26

he had set himself an impossible task and might yet be faced with a humiliating climbdown.

Dermot read Tania Aebi's book *Maiden Voyage* and was amazed at how a young girl without any real sailing background could circumnavigate the world. He assured himself that if she could succeed with her limited experience then he could certainly sail the Atlantic single-handed. He could see the sense in his own argument but there were times when he felt that people such as her were in another league. He could not see that even achievers struggled with the fear of failure to reach the winner's podium. Dare he drag a foot from the mire of his own insecurities to step a little higher?

When not working on *Poitín* he studied navigation and read any publication which he thought could be of benefit. A local sea captain helped with the study of celestial navigation and assured him that within a 'few days' of putting to sea he would master the subject. Dermot was confused as to how he was supposed to manage between departing and a 'few days' later.

He put *Poitín* back in the water and practised sailing her alone in the hope of building up confidence in single-handed sailing. Having sailed for many years he knew how to handle a boat in most coastal situations but being alone demanded he became more alert and establish a rhythm with the sea. Without crew to sail the boat and keep watch while he slept he knew that hightened senses would be needed to avoid getting into trouble.

He got the crazy notion of jumping over the side with the harness on, while the boat was sailing, to practise pulling himself back on board. But knowing the effort required to scoop a bucket of water, when washing down the decks, he always found an excuse not to try the man overboard exercise. The truth was he suspected that such a fright might cause him to cancel the trip, sell the boat, and take up something more sedate. Worse still he considered the possibility of actually drowning before ever departing and the local rescue services being called out 'to assist some gobshite trying to ski barefoot behind a yacht'. Somehow it made more sense to rely on adrenalin in the event of the situation ever arising rather than make a complete fool of himself in Arklow Bay.

When at last he considered that most precautions had been taken and that *Poitín* was adequately prepared, he relaxed, put aside all the disastrous scenarios and tried as best he could to envisage the excitement and fun the voyage would doubtlessly have to offer.

When he first told his parents of his true plans they were understandably concerned but accepted it was his life to do as he wished. He wondered if his mother knew how much she was to blame for him wanting to attempt such a voyage. From an early age she nurtured in her children a sense of adventure. Through her love of reading he was introduced to such people as Scott of the Antarctic, Sir Francis Chichester, Naomi James and so many others. She admired their courage and sowed the belief that adventurers were honest and noble people. She backed up her words with actions, regularly taking her children for hikes in the Wicklow Mountains. Stories of her own childhood adventures spent in those very same mountains, on those very same treks, aroused pride. He was the son of an adventurer whose images invoked the strongest of emotions that quietly took seed in the fertile soil of a young heart.

In contrast, his father preferred to look to sporting competition and business achievers of the day, and being extremely ambitious, rose to the head of every organisation and club he ever joined. If Dermot acquired a sense of adventure from his mother, it was his father who instilled the dogged determination to succeed wherever he set his mind. Although he considered Dermot too old for such an irresponsible voyage, he secretly relished the opportunity.

Since returning from Australia father and son had grown a little closer but the protective barriers which Dermot erected during childhood remained firmly in place. He expected criticism from his father as if he were still a schoolboy and the slightest remark that something he had done was not correct incurred the coolest of snubs.

It is sometimes hard to believe the profound effect the simplest of childhood experiences can have on adult life. The relationship between father and son faltered at a very early age, which was mainly due to Dermot's attitude to school. He could not see the sense in devoting so much time and effort to schoolwork when there were boyhood adventures to be enjoyed. Like most children he spent a great deal of time alone living out his dreams. He was always the hero in his exploits, imagining himself to be brave, while taking chances the other kids were too scared to risk.

They lived by the sea in a quiet country area where he explored the far-off hills and headlands in exciting lone expeditions. On a few occasions he managed to persuade his school friends to join him but the excitement of distant headlands did not justify the long hike. They also feared being punished for straying too far from home, something to which Dermot had grown accustomed. At least when he was out there on his own he was free to live a few hours without the restrictions of school and his father's frustrated efforts to teach him to spell. He knew how to spell 'b-r-e-a-d' but every time he stood in front of the bread bin he froze. No matter how hard his father tried, or how many times he shouted in frustration, Dermot could not or would not spell that word. As soon as his father left the kitchen his mother would very calmly coax him to spell 'b-r-e-a-d' and he could do it without any real problem. He responded to her tenderness and craved the hug and affection with which she rewarded him, far more than he feared the ear bashing his father threatened.

The man was determined to see his son succeed in school and find 'an easier way of making a living' but the more he pushed, the more entrenched Dermot became in his refusal to learn. He could not understand why the schoolwork from a teacher his parents hardly knew mattered more than his happiness. Why could he not be loved for just being himself? If only his father could have played with him in his dream world he would have seen how different he was. He would have seen that he was brave and strong and noble just like him. He adored the ground his father walked on and sought his love regardless of whether or not he could spell 'b-r-e-a-d'.

Dermot hoped he would one day be just like his father, strong and handsome but above all, proud. Not that he really understood what pride was at that age. All he knew was that his father had an air about him that he longed for.

More than anything else he wanted to please him and have his praise, but he went about it the wrong way. The more he tried to do the right thing in his 'dream world', the more his schoolwork suffered and the more his father despaired. He was punished for his lack of learning but soon it became apparent he was far too stubborn to respond to a spanking. He was offered his father's best pocket knife if he learned multiplication tables. Dermot grasped the numbers with surprising ease and his father was greatly relieved to discover his son was not stupid – 'there, you see, you can do it when you want to.'

Dermot began picturing the feast of goodies to be earned from doing that stupid homework but soon realised that it was expected of him once he had shown his potential. His mother pleaded and his father tried spanking him, more out of frustration than any desire to punish his darling boy. Assurances from his mother that his father still loved him and wanted only the best for his son confused his innocent mind.

The fact that his father adored him and tried to hide it for the sake of his schoolwork only added to his confusion. While his sister and brother preferred to stay at home and play, he used go for drives in the car with 'his Dad'. Dermot loved being seen with him and relished every moment spent in his company.

But eventually all that changed with his refusal to learn. He began avoiding their outings because the conversation inevitably led to schoolwork. His father felt rejected by the beautiful young son he so loved while Dermot grew to accept he had disappointed the greatest father any little boy could have wished for in the world.

The relationship between them deteriorated steadily over the years, which was the greatest of tragedies as they could so easily have become the closest of friends. Neither knew how to return to the early childhood days of fun and affection before that cursed bread bin came between them. Dermot drifted through school, an erratic performer who was somewhat confused and increasingly ashamed of his results. In an effort to encourage him to work harder, his father praised his schoolfriends and told him how proud their fathers were of their results. He desperately wanted to help him achieve but instead Dermot felt hurt and even more ashamed. The sense of shame turned to anger and resentment, which drove a wedge two decades thick between them. Dermot's anger passed from his mind into the depths of his soul, and in the process turned on himself.

Between Instinct and Luck

The excitement of the moment helped control the blind anxiety that welled up inside. As he manoeuvred *Poitín* through the fleet of yachts moored in the river, he thought how much safer it would be to stay at home and enjoy the midweek races or weekend cruises to nearby ports. As if a last ditch temptation by 'the demon of doubt', his mind flashed a glimpse of *Poitín* in the hostile expanse of the Atlantic Ocean. And while he considered the safety of Arklow Harbour the demon sniggered 'you are not the sort of person to undertake an adventure like this ... the next step is outside your league ... it's not too late ...'

'You bastard,' he grunted through snared teeth. 'Don't you dare do this to me now. This is where you get out of my life,' spitting the fear from his mouth.

Jumping to his feet, desperate to regain control, he pleaded, 'Please God, help me through this, help me let go.'

Slowly, very slowly, his surroundings came into focus. The early morning calm passed over his heart, quelling the doubts and restoring self-belief. Through the calm he recognised how the decision to set sail had long since been made and it was now simply a matter of getting on with it all. What he had put in motion was based on months of planning and years of preparation. He had waited too long for this opportunity to be tricked by fear.

In an attempt to control the milling thoughts, he began

making a mental list of every piece of equipment and publication which he would need over the coming year. Until such time as *Poitín* returned to Arklow, she was his home, his travelling companion and his refuge from the ocean. She was already loaded down with supplies, charts, books and equipment, yet there remained even more paraphernalia to acquire along the way. He thought about Gibraltar where he hoped to stock-up, and tried to picture being moored in the shadow of 'The Rock'. A proud smile came to his face and he began to feel positive and enthusiastic.

The beauty of the summer's morning lured him from his imaginings. Gentle puffs of cloud floated across a vivid blue sky not yet veiled by the heat of the day. A yawning sun glanced sideways upon the commercial harbour, casting cool shadows from imposing quays onto the water below. *Poitín* moved between shadow and light, blinking her way towards the open sea. High above the fishing boats which had not yet put to sea, seagulls vied for position, hoping to dive on discarded breakfast scraps. Most of the fleet had departed hours earlier leaving only a handful to make final repairs or wait on crews dragging weekend hangovers.

Poitín's little single-cylinder sought credit for the river's flow which carried her along – exhaust sounds stomping across the water, then up the quaysides in search of attention. An old fisherman, attracted by the flickering noise, paused for a moment from repairing nets and tossed a wave in *Poitín*'s direction. Like a feeding gull, his hand swooped with open fingers to pluck a smouldering fag from its bearded nest. The hidden mouth then shouted what looked like 'a-be-au-ty-of-a-day'. Dermot responded with an overly-enthusiastic wave and big nervous smile which left the old boy unsure. Weather-beaten eyes were suddenly lost as confused wrinkles washed across his face and a tilt of the head demanded to know more.

Dermot's attempt to mime, 'Bay of Biscay, Canary Islands, Atlantic ... me ... solo', foundered en route across the water. He wanted the whole harbour to know he was doing something special but old harbours such as Arklow are more concerned with safe returns than fancy declarations.

Poitín carried on regardless of the theatrics.

Once they had left the shelter of the harbour an early morning breeze greeted them on its way down the coast. Snippets of wind, strong enough to ruffle the loose silk strewn across the bay, allowed him to turn off the engine. A pleased silence rushed to fill the void and *Poitín* drifted mindlessly across the surface. He set about hoisting the big genoa and main; sheeting in the sails, she heeled slightly, then settled down to a steady three knots. The automatic tiller-pilot seemed to hold her safely on course which opened an opportunity to go below and make a cup of tea.

Cup in hand, he tried to remember what he had forgotten or left undone. '*Poitín, Poitín, Poitín*, this is ...' voiced from the VHF radio. He reached across the table, eager to answer the call. 'Yes Barry, go ahead,' he said, noticing the tremble in his hand. A confidant from the sailing club had watched *Poitín* depart and waited until the worst was over before calling to say 'bon voyage' and assure him of his ability to cope alone. Those few words from a yachtsman whose experience he respected helped his confidence to take hold.

Poitín headed off down the east coast of Ireland carrying her cargo of dreams and aspirations. It was the sort of day sailors pray for; clear sky, fresh breeze and a favourable weather forecast. Perfect conditions in which to ease into the voyage.

As the morning progressed the wind filled-in and with an ebb tide in their favour they soon clocked up the miles. As if *Poitín* knew that it was more than just another short sail along the coast she skipped across the water filling him with her enthusiasm. All the worries and anxieties were now left behind in Arklow and he danced around the boat feeling the tingle of sun and sea that filled the air. Boogeying on the fore-deck, he screamed with delight. Yipping and yoo-hooing with relief and excitement, harnessed like a mischievous child, he laughed at how ridiculous he must have looked.

Invigorated by the smooth departure and refreshed from the little war dance around the foredeck, he eventually settled down and began preparing *Poitín* for the dangers that lay ahead. A maze of channels wound their way through the unseen sandbanks which he had opted to navigate. With each change of tide came a frantic rush of water through the banks, but weather permitting, it was a powerful force which could be used to advantage. Having sailed the east coast on many occasions he had an intimate respect for the dangers which lay in ambush for opportunities. The Blackwater Bank, The Rusk Channel, The Lucifer Bank, all were names associated with wrecked ships and loss of life at sea.

Dermot's earlier intoxication gave way to common sense. He began to pay special attention to the charts and navigational buoys which marked a narrow channel through the web of submerged dunes.

The wind freshened to 30 knots as a single Cardinal Buoy came into view marking the entrance to the banks. He prepared *Poitín* for the Rusk Channel while only a short distance away white caps began breaking on the shallow ground. The fresh wind drove *Poitín* towards the entrance at over six knots while underneath, the bulging tide funnelled through the channel at a frantic rate.

Waves began breaking on either side like short, sharp outbursts from a bad-tempered tide which resented the bank's restraints. He risked losing control, with little room for error. While the self-steering held *Poitín* on course he managed to reduce sail just as the wind increased even further.

He soon regained control of the situation without too much loss of speed and within 30 minutes *Poitín* was squirted through the narrows and clear of immediate danger. He knew he should have opted for a slower and safer passage on the outside of the banks but that would have offered only a fraction of the thrill. The experience reminded him of the dangerous excitement of white-water canoeing, except the craft now measured nine metres and the shore was a long way off.

The wind remained fresh all afternoon as he sailed south towards Rosslare Harbour. Knowing there was ample room in which to manoeuvre he relaxed and enjoyed the sight of the distant coast. He had played on those sandy beaches as a child, and passed many a happy summer on 'Old Town', only a few miles inland. He had assumed that because his grandparents were old the farm had been named after them.

Grandad O'Neill, the father of his father, the giant's giant, was surely the biggest man in all of Ireland, if not the whole wide world. He could certainly have laid claim to being the kindest but it was not in his gentle nature to do so. Without the responsibility of parenthood, the old man lavished unrestrained affection on his doting grandchild. Beside the kitchen range, a two-seater couch harboured defiant springs that fought boyhood bounces with avengeance. Before settling into his high-backed wooden chair with newspaper and pipe, the old man would take a turn on the springs. Caught off balance, the boy was swept onto his grandfather's lap for a vigorous tickling. Enormous hands tossed and rolled the playful pup. Gasping for air, the boy inhaled smells deep into his memory, far deeper than any cautious sniff. Musty summer smells, of harvest and animals, of farmyard dogs and pipe tobacco. Funny how panting dogs would always remind him of block-tobacco, of grandfather, of childhood summers, and happy times before school and cursed b-r-e-a-d bins.

Rosslare Head appeared as an island on the silver afternoon horizon. As usual the surrounding low-lying shore remained hidden until the last minute, a trick which sometimes instilled confusion on first arrival. Dermot had been caught out years before and the memory still served as a reminder to heed logic before perception.

Poitín arrived at the harbour entrance around five o'clock. A few people stood on the bridge of the B&I Car Ferry observing the antics on *Poitín* as he hurried about, taking down sails and preparing to enter port. He waited for the enormous white 'block-of-flats' to dock, spellbound by the precision of the manoeuvre. *Poitín*, a single bedsit by comparison, slipped into the fishing harbour round the back.

A local trawlerman allowed him to tie up alongside, 'so long as you're out of the way by half six tomorrow morning'. Between passing lines and adjusting fenders they nudged into conversation. The local man proved to be a hive of information; a detailed weather forecast could be obtained from the local meteorological office and a good pint of stout was served in the pub overlooking the harbour, which also had live music every Thursday night.

Dermot liked this man – he seemed like a decent hard-working fellow who made a living from what was one of the most dangerous corners of the Atlantic. The man eyed the 'toy boat' that lay alongside his 60-foot trawler. 'Why do you want to make it any harder than it already is?' he asked, confused as to why anyone would want to sail alone in such a small boat. Dermot felt silly, even spoilt to be so indulgent with life. A light-hearted offer of madness in his own defence was readily accepted by the man who returned to his nets, shaking his head in confusion. 'Jay-sus ... should be locked up.'

After tidying the boat, Dermot went ashore to buy fresh milk and bread for the passage south to Land's End, on the West coast of England. The next leg of the trip involved 120 miles across strong tidal waters and he needed to be sure of good weather. The meteorological office gave the all-clear for the next couple of days which was sufficient justification for a celebratory pint. From the bar high above the harbour he watched the bustle of cars and container trucks preparing to board the ferry. In the corner of the inner harbour was *Poitín*, nestled up against the ocean trawler like a suckling calf. He felt good about his first day, a safe passage with a little bit of excitement to add to proceedings. He knew he had become too anxious sailing through the banks but that was his nature – maybe it would help keep trouble at bay later in the voyage.

The following morning he woke to the roar of the big diesel engines as the trawler prepared to depart. The few pints from the night before had helped him to sleep later than expected. He stuck his head out the hatch and nodded to the skipper who indicated in no uncertain terms that he had ten minutes in which to move out of the way. Before departing, the skipper quietly offered a bag of ice, 'to keep a few drinks cold', and wished him luck alone on the ocean. The trawler's departure left an ugly quay wall plastered with truck tires and oil. A boat anchored nearby offered a better location to moor *Poitín* and enjoy breakfast while waiting for the tide to change.

By 07.40 he had slipped lines and *Poitín* made her way across a mercury surface which heaved gently as if restraining movement below. Still air, with patches of early morning mist, waited for the breeze to wake from its slumber. A sigh was all that was required to get things moving.

Poitín motored for a few hours until well clear of the harbour. The weather forecast was for light winds, which meant for a slow passage, but at least there was six hours of ebb tide in his favour. In that time he hoped to get far enough south of the Irish coast to avoid the worst of the flood tide which would push north for another six hours.

The high-pressure weather system that hung over the area provided a beautiful clear blue sky but very little wind for sailing. He preferred to turn off the engine as soon as possible after leaving port and enjoy the peace and calm of the boat as she sailed quietly through the water. But on this occasion he felt it was better to push on under motor and clock up the miles.

Two hours out to sea *Poitín* slipped past Tuskar Rock Lighthouse which stood like an enormous white candle wedged into the sea. Molten swells flopped on the protruding rocks and occasionaly broke in patches of white as though wax dripped from above. A few porpoises appeared and came to play alongside *Poitín*. Wet and gleaming in the morning sun, they filled their lungs with the cool clean air and arched their backs to dive time and time again under *Poitín*'s bow. With exacting speed and grace of movement they planted the gentlest of kisses on *Poitín*'s cheek, rushed away when detected, and coyly waited for approval before daring to return. Their performance delighted him and he showed his appreciation by leaning over the bow and cheering each time they appeared. He always took it as a good omen when dolphins or porpoises choose to play alongside the boat. Their eyes seemed almost human, as if understanding his apprehension for the voyage ahead and willing him on his way. As the sun rose higher a light wind began to blow and Dermot was at last free to turn off the engine. The boat trickled along under sail as he set about preparing lunch and making a mental list of chores to do around the boat.

Taking the midday sun sight with the sextant appeared straightforward at first, exactly as Danny had shown him back in Arklow but the completed calculations gave a position 300 miles away, somewhere off the North coast of Spain. Repeated sights resulted in similar positions and he appreciated why it might take a 'day or two' to master the instrument. With a hand-held Radio Direction Finder on board the sextant was not yet critical to his navigation and he opted to 'dead reckon' his way to England. In the meantime practice was definitely called for with the sextant.

After lunch he wrote up the Log, then listened to the radio: the news, a chat show, much the same news again on-the-hour and a quiz show that sent him off to sleep. Two questions later, he sat bolt upright, certain he had slept for hours. Feeling restless he decided to rearrange the cockpit locker to help pass the time. Having emptied the entire contents onto the cockpit floor, he then sorted everything and returned it to the locker in a new order of importance. Halfway through the process, he noticed a loose electrical wire which had inadvertently been pulled from the back of the ignition switch. He connected it to what he felt sure was the correct terminal and turned the key to check that the switch was working properly. All seemed well without actually starting the engine so he turned off the ignition and continued packing the locker.

The morning breeze carried him as far as mid-afternoon and then continued on its way leaving him becalmed. He waited for the next puff to arrive, more out of discipline than patience but ten pages later of Steinbeck's best saw him up on deck taking down the head sail. It was time to start the engine.

With not a ship in sight, he settled down once again to enjoy a cup of coffee and continue with the gentle detail of Lennie's mouse. Sometime later he re-read the last paragraph, worried he had missed something important. He smelt burning and turned from the pages to see the cabin filled with thick black smoke. He froze, unable to believe the horror of what he saw. Then as if in slow-motion-replay realised, 'Christ, the boat's on fire!' Black smoke bellowed from the cockpit, foul toxic fumes as if from a factory chimney. His mind, confused and disorientated, failed him. The boat no longer resembled *Poitín* – everything had changed.

'Where ...? How ...? Somebody do ...'

'Stop ... think,' he shouted as he somehow slowed his mind sufficiently to think. There was no fire to be seen. 'Why no flames?'

He turned off the engine and took a deep breath before diving into the black of the cabin. His eyes very quickly began to burn as he searched the galley area, but there were no flames to be found. He clambered out on deck, gasping for air and grabbed the fire extinguisher on the way. A few quick breaths of clean air. He jumped below again to remove part of the engine cover but could see nothing through the thick murky smoke. His lungs heaved as he burst out into the cockpit, nearly dropped the fire extinguisher, inhaled filth on the way, coughed and choked, eyes semi-focused through the streaming tears. A vile taste filled his mouth and a strange stinging occupied his chest. He stood gasping to clear his lungs and began to feel dizzy.

The near-full tank of diesel and two gas cylinders could explode at any moment but he dare not use the only fire extinguisher until such time as he had flames to fight. There was a logical way of handling the situation but he could not think straight. Fear taunted, reminding him he was alone at sea and that his boat was on fire. He could feel the first rumblings of panic in the pit of his stomach.

'Think man, think. What next?'

He had no choice but to stay with the boat and try to fight the fire, wherever it might be. Just as he was about to dive into the nightmare of the cabin once more, the faintest snippet of an inner voice prompted '... the cockpit locker'. As he lifted the lid, black smoke billowed from the locker but quickly cleared to reveal the cause of the problem. The electrical wires connected to the ignition switch had overheated to such an extent that the plastic insulation had begun to bubble and smoulder.

With the battery turned off, he waited anxiously to see if the wires cooled or burst into flames. First the smoke began to clear from the cabin and then the fumes. The worst was over. He released his stranglehold on the fire extinguisher and felt his knees turn to jelly. He flopped onto the seat and stared at his shaking hands. Some time passed before his breathing slowed and his mind began to grasp the full extent of what had happened.

'Jesus ... that was close.'

He remembered the hip flask his sister had given him, 'for emergencies only' and with the help of a swig tried to identify what had gone wrong. He had ignored his intuition earlier in the day when cleaning out the cockpit locker and reconnected the wrong wire to the ignition switch. The whispers warned that all was not well as he proceeded with the chores but were dismissed. Another warning crossed his mind around lunch time but by late afternoon the whispers had died with the wind.

Some time elapsed before he brought himself to consider getting under way again. After inspecting the situation he decided to take the fan belt off the alternator and start the engine by hand. The single cylinder ticked over nicely, and after a final check, slipped her into gear and continued on his way. Without the alternator connected, he needed to conserve electrical power but knew there was enough in the batteries to leave the navigation lights on over night.

As the day drew to a close, the wind died and the sky clouded over, bringing with it damp cold air that made the flat sea appear a little less friendly. Any passing ships or fishing boats stood a good chance of seeing *Poitín*'s masthead light in the good visibility. With the sails down he decided to let *Poitín* drift on the tide and tried to get some sleep. He lay on the cabin floor in the hope of hearing the engine sounds or the propellers of approaching ships should they come too close. It was his first night at sea alone, a new experience and another little test.

Dermot was still too anxious after the day's events to sleep and woke continualy throughout the night, imagining he had overslept and was heading into trouble. He would rush out into the cockpit only to find that his was the only boat on the black expanse of water. A voice whispered, 'all is well ... sleep ... trust yourself', but was lost to the chatter of the 'what if's that filled his mind with re-enactments of the day's mishaps.

Numerous cups of tea and a corned-beef sandwich later, the night sea was broken by specks of light, probably a fishing fleet of five or six boats, which didn't come very close. A few large navigation lights entered the night arena and kept him busy trying to identify on what course they were headed. Within an hour of their arrival all the lights were gone and he was left with the darkness. He curled up in the corner of the cockpit, pulled the jacket hood over his head and fell into a deep sleep.

Twenty minutes later, maybe half an hour, he woke as the sun prepared to pour into the day. The morning had thrown open its shutters and in the distance vessels spiked the horizon like winter trees on a desolate land. With the dawn came a hint of breeze, fickle at first and lacking enthusiam, yet enough to keep his attention. A pre-emptive hoisting of sails consolidated the breeze and carried *Poitín* off at a steady three knots.

The morning passed slowly as he lay in the cockpit enjoying the sailing and the gentle rhythm of the boat. After breakfast he checked the navigation and lay outside with the gentle sun upon his skin. The radio played from the cabin and he drifted in and out of sleep.

A massive explosion ripped through the air. His eyes flashed open as a second bang resounded across the sky. He jumped to his feet and checked the cabin but all was in order. Scanning the sky for distress flares, he saw nothing. Then he remembered something about a British Naval exercise area and was about to check the chart when he recalled a friend's warning about the noise Concord made when breaking the sound barrier. He settled back into the cockpit and tried to relax, accepting that he was not under attack from Her Majesty's Navy. 'If the first two days are anything to go by,' he thought, 'how the hell am I ever going to make it across the Atlantic?'

At first, only a distant headland was visible through the evening haze. *Poitín* trickled along, and between her and Penzance lay Land's End with its tentacles of off-lying rocks. He had hoped to make port by nightfall but that was before the fire and the fickle winds of the past twelve hours. The prospect of a good night's sleep while safely tied up in Penzance harbour was dangerously inviting. His tide calculations were influenced by enthusiasm rather than prudence and he opted to round the head rather than wait till morning. *Poitín* drifted off to starboard as if she had heard his intuition pleading and was fearful of the decision but the helmsman noticed nothing unusual, heard nothing, and forced her back on course.

An hour later he realised that soon after rounding the lighthouse, the tide would change and *Poitín* risked being swept back across the rocks. With the wind barely filling her sails and a tiny engine, there was no way that she could fight the flooding tide. He checked the chart and decided to take advantage of the slack water between the change of tides to steer for a cove on the near side of the headland.

Poitín began her dash for Whitesand Bay as daylight faded. He knew he was breaking a basic rule of sailing by attempting to enter an unlit bay at night but tiredness prompted him to take a chance. The chart showed a clear passage but he wondered if it contained sufficient detail to justify such crazy action. Motor sailing, he headed straight for the cove on the last snippet of light, watching for rocks or any sign of tidal drift. The wind seemed to stiffen and drove *Poitín* faster through unseen hazards. He spilled the main but feared not making the cove before the change of tide. There was no turning back and no time to slow down. The markings by which he had set his course were no longer visible. A transit was set between instinct and luck.

Feeling he was safe from the tidal stream, he slowed *Poitín* to a crawl and nudged her towards the shallow water near the beach. As the depth sounder touched the five metre mark, he dropped the anchor and thanked his lucky stars for the safety of the cove. A chance had been taken and the gods had shown their favour but he promised there could never, ever be a next time.

Escaping danger left the sweetest aftertaste of invincibility. He faced the stars and roared with laughter, his fists clenched tightly, strangling the 'what if's that sought to be heard. He decided the skipper was not to be scolded, for no other life had been put in danger. 'My decision, my life to risk,' he thought.

With the moon low in the night sky he sat outside enjoying a hot meal and wondered if he had embarked on the adventure of a lifetime or a series of near disasters which would lead to his eventual insanity. He imagined *Poitín* being turned away from some Caribbean island to protect the inhabitants from the lunatic skipper, and laughed aloud.

All in all, it had been a very eventful start to his single-handed sailing but he was safe and well, with little to complain about. He questioned his ability to complete the voyage, based on the performances over the last two days, but dismissed the mishaps as teething problems which would not recur.

Any negative thoughts soon drifted from his mind as he watched the moon rise above the high cliffs and fill the bay with its light. *Poitín* was safely positioned for the night and the weather forecast offered more of the same. The alarm was set for the next change of tide when he would need to check the anchor. Having taken a chance to find a safe anchorage for the night, the last thing he wanted was to be carried onto the rocks while he slept.

***

The morning sky greeted him clear and blue. He sat in the cockpit eating breakfast and observed the beautiful sandy bay with its seagulls soaring on the shadowed cliff face to the north. Perched on crystal clear water, *Poitín* rocked from side to side, a metronome pulsing to the gentle roll of the sea. With the morning sun on his back, he felt a surge of self-contained strength, a warm sense of achievement. Without help from another soul he had sailed his little boat 130 miles and had coped with mishaps along the way. Each day was a new step forward and a personal best. This was what he had hoped to discover alone at sea, but failed to see the belief needed to set sail from Arklow. He clung to the moment, fearing this confidence might ebb on the next tide.

Feet on a Sea of Prayer

After breakfast Dermot checked the navigation and prepared *Poitín* to depart. The sail around Land's End to Penzance was an absolute joy with a fresh breeze and strong tide in his favour. *Poitín* swept past the south coast of Cornwall at eight knots. The sea was a minefield of lobster pots and fishing nets and it seemed the decision not to round the headland at night was the lesser of two evils.

It was not long after morning coffee when he sighted Penzance town. He checked the chart and set about navigating an approach to the harbour entrance. According to the pilot book the inner harbour could only be entered on high tide when the lock gates were opened. With three hours to kill he dropped anchor and waited for the tide to elevate *Poitín* to the level of the boats which floated on the skyline overhead.

It was hard to imagine the enormous gates opening with anything other than a torrent of water, yet when the time came they yielded to the ocean with the sweetest little eddies. *Poitín* slipped into the magic pond, and as instructed by the harbour master, lay alongside an old wooden boat.

He went ashore to clear customs, and checked at the harbour office if there was somewhere he might shower. He liked the look of Penzance, a lovely old seafaring town, a feel of Kinsale to it. Listening to the accents of the local people, he tried to imagine the Penzance of old, with its pirates and sailing ships.

Basic but clean was how the ablution block presented itself. Tucked in his hand were enough coins for a double session in the shower – it was time for a treat. He wasted not a minute in ridding his body of the clothes which clung, salty and damp. The introductory cold water lasted to the edge of concern, then bowed to the power of the electric metre. His fingers tested, 'ah, too hot' – a new mix and wait.

Perfect body temperature lured him, hands first, into a warm seductive spray. Absolute heaven cascaded onto closed eyes leaching salt from pores, the smell of toxic smoke from thick dry hair. Herbal shampoo's sweet aroma. The gentle feel of lather between hand and skin. Pensive muscles relaxed and sighed. Such relief.

Lost in his aquatic heaven, an eternity passed before the metre clicked one last time and the plumbing hummed to a different sound. Cold water surged through the pipes, eager to regain control of the spray. He braced himself. Frantic movements of the hands struggled to disperse the shock. His shivering body. Then the tingle of cold skin taut on warm muscles. Enough.

Like most harbours, Penzance had a central roosting place which attracted a menagerie of mariners, located in the sunniest, most sheltered corner. With a prime view of all movements, they sat and observed. Selective aloofness ensured they remained in control and lent a sense of authority to the bench. Sometimes they invited fresh input from strangers but never so much as to risk the integrity of the group, for a place on the harbour bench was a sacred thing.

He passed the group on the way into town and acknowledged their importance with an upward nod of the head. One of the old characters folded his arms and called to Dermot.

'Oi, you be from Ireland then?' he said in a deep Cornish accent, which at first sounded like a take-off from a Hollywood pirate movie.

'Yes, from Arklow. On the East coast.'

'Arrrh, Arklow, you must know George then, George off *'ether Bell,'* by way of statement rather than question.

'Yes I do,' he said, surprised to cast his mind back to Arklow. 'I used crew on the Lifeboat with him.'

'Good man. Well, you tell George I'ws askin' after 'im,' he said offering his own name in reverse order.

'OK, but I won't see him for at least a year. I'm sailing to the West Indies.'

'Don't ye worry 'bout that me 'ansome, you just tell 'im when you sees 'im.'

Shit, thought Dermot, no big deal about my solo trans-Atlantic trip here.

It was thanks to George that *Poitín* and he were made feel so welcome in Penzance. As a solitary person he offered no threat to the bench and was welcomed without reserve. Always a friendly word for the new arrival, even time to chat, whenever he passed. They helped organise an electrician to repair *Poitín*'s wiring and offered general advice, not all of which was taken on board.

Having replaced the burnt-out electrical wires and corrected the error on the ignition switch, he considered the passage from Rosslare. The patter of rain broke the evening silence of the harbour. Supper dishes lay to one side and a candle flickered broken light on the Atlantic chart spread before him. Arklow and Penzance seemed frighteningly close together, as if in the same bay. Much closer than four days sailing. He pondered the Atlantic undertaking.

After nearly a week Dermot felt relaxed in the familiarity of the safe surroundings and was reluctant to leave when *Poitín* was ready for sea. He was last through the harbour gates on the morning of departure and received a knowing look from the bench gang. The old boy who knew George walked to the quayside as *Poitín* passed.

'You be careful out there,' he said and sauntered back to the bench.

The trip to the Isles of Scilly was short and enjoyable. With over 100 islands and off-lying rocks, not to mention a seven-knot current, making the right approach to the islands was critical. A lazy summer haze which shrouded the distant black humps in a sameness made navigation difficult. An old Radio Direction Finder (RDF) which he borrowed for the voyage came into its own – a simple but effective device which operated on radio signals transmitted from certain headlands, lighthouses and harbours.

He checked the RDF bearing before calculating a course for the approach to the islands. Once in the main channel he felt safe and followed the navigational buoys marking the path through Saint Mary's Sound. As he had expected, the ebb tide made the going slow and offered no alternative but to relax and enjoy the view.

Boats taking advantage of the good weather and holiday weekend crowded Saint Mary's bay. *Poitín* sailed through the bobbing craft in search of a suitable place in which to anchor. Back and forth he sailed until a clearing beckoned on the far edge of the fleet. *Poitín* rounded-up into the wind, slowed, then stopped a few metres astern of a motor boat. He stepped quickly to the bow and checked the position relative to the surrounding boats. As *Poitín* fell away from the wind, he fed out the anchor chain until sufficient length was set for the depth below. He then backed the head sail to put reverse pressure on the anchor and waited to see if it held. When all seemed in order, he dropped the sails, and to his surprise, received applause from the people on a boat nearby. He nodded and smiled in appreciation, knowing from experience how unusual it was to have anyone take notice when a sailing manoeuvre went well.

Feeling content with himself for a passage without mishaps, he moved about the boat smiling as he bagged sails and prepared to stay a day or two in port. A burst of laughter from the nearby audience echoed through his head as uncertainty. He looked around *Poitín* in search of failure but all seemed well. A quick glance in their direction and he felt the anger grow. They chatted among themselves and it was obvious the joke did not involve him. He had allowed himself to jump to the wrong conclusion. His sudden anger gave way to a sense of disappointment. 'That was a perfect sailing manoeuvre, why couldn't you just accept the credit?'

He set about sorting out the boat, putting sailing items away while unpacking those bits and pieces needed when in port. He intended staying for a few days to allow a frontal weather system time to pass. High Town was the only village on the islands, with a thriving tourist business that revolved around the harbour. Open wooden boats, busy ferrying people back and forth to the surrounding islands on sight-seeing trips dodged the steady stream of tenders which plied between the moored yachts and the slipway at the far end of the stone pier. The holiday weekend business injected Saint Mary's with a life-saving transfusion which would help it through the quiet winter months.

Poitín felt tranquil and content to be among the other boats as he lounged in the cockpit enjoying a cup of tea. With the electrical problem repaired and the alternator working again, there was ample power to play the cassette unit. A familiar tape that reminded him of good times helped to take the edge off travelling alone. Van Morisson's mixture of groan, grunt and repetitious ramblings, even song, drifted through, lending a happy ambience to the new surroundings. 'No one can moan, can moan, can moan, can moan, like Van,' he thought.

Dermot slept well and late, waking around nine o'clock. Cooking breakfast and eating, then coffee with a two-day old newspaper kept him occupied. Soon after midday the Harbour Master came to collect mooring fees and advised him to expect a call from the police who were preparing for a Royal visit to the islands. Later in the day, two officers came by asking to see his passport, even though he had cleared customs in Penzance. The boat's papers appeared to be in order but there remained a few questions – questions asked in such a way as to say 'we know you are guilty of something' – the very same technique used by police the world over to unsettle the guilty and warn the innocent to stay in line. When it was obvious he posed no security threat, they relaxed and chatted about *Poitín* and the voyage ahead.

One afternoon when checking the rigging in preparation to depart, the skipper from a Swedish yacht came by asking for information regarding the Irish Coast. The Swede was heading home to Stockholm, via Ireland, after two years of cruising the Atlantic. Dermot offered him the use of *Poitín's* mooring should he visit Arklow and in return was told where to find a free mooring in Gibraltar. Having recently cruised the coasts of Spain and Portugal he had plenty of useful tips for Dermot. After nearly two hours of friendly chat and a few beers the Swede departed. It was Dermot's first insight into the pilgrimage of yachts around the Atlantic and the camaraderie which exists between them.

He updated his charts and pilot books with the information acquired from the Swede and prepared a passage plan for the next leg of the journey. His original intention was to head straight across the English Channel for Spain but he had been persuaded that the French island of Ouessant was worth visiting. Most of the commercial traffic for Northern Europe passed through the busy shipping lanes off Ouessant. It was critical that he confronted this danger in daylight.

***

The weather forecast for Wednesday 30 May was for light winds, which promised a slow trip across the Channel. Ideally it should have taken twenty hours to make the 100-mile passage to

Ouessant, but with light winds he estimated on being at sea for much longer. Approaching the island from the west was essential so as not to get caught in the rip tides which swept over the foul ground to the east. Once the summer heat haze was established, identifying the shoreline would be difficult. By departing Saint Mary's early the next day he hoped to be sufficiently close to Ouessant before sunrise to take a bearing off the lighthouse loom and avoid getting too close to any unseen dangers.

As planned he departed after breakfast, allowing an hour to motor through Saint Mary's Sound and out into the open sea. In a short while, he expected the ebb tide to pick up and carry *Poitín* in a south-west direction towards her destination. Loose cloth lay crumpled on deck waiting for the transformation to swollen sail which only wind could effect. It was shaping up to be another scorcher of a day, nothing else for him to do but push on under motor in hope of the afternoon breeze.

The horizon, speckled with trawlers, offered distant company while *Poitín* chugged along to the rhythm of the diesel engine. Her wake pointed back to the morning and the islands which lay hidden behind the global curve. The promised afternoon wind took its time arriving but had the courtesy to delay its departure until late into the evening.

By midnight *Poitín* was once again becalmed. The wind's exit, like a shuffling congregation, left a monastic silence hanging in the air. Ripples appeared on a dark polished floor, as undulations worn by holy feet on an endless sea of prayer. He sat patiently waiting for the quieter sounds, a backwash from the first waves of silence.

Only halfway across the English Channel and it was obvious he would not keep to the original timetable. He desperately wanted to have the security of Ouessant light to steer by, to confirm his position, to keep him company, but it was nowhere to be seen. Something lurked in the back of his mind, waiting to catch him off guard. He began to feel unsure of what he was doing at that moment in life. Tired and vulnerable, he was in no shape for cross-examination and knew the only defence was sleep.

Well away from Ouessant and the shipping lanes which rounded the island to the north was as good a place as any to lay his head upon a pillow. Again he decided it made sense to lie on the floor in the hope of hearing ships through the stillness of the night. But anxiety overcame his belief in the warning system and he slept for only ten or fifteen minutes at a time. What sleep he did manage was spattered with nightmares of *Poitín* being rammed by a passing ship.

The wind picked up a little by 07:30 the next morning and he hoisted sails hoping to make Ouessant by early afternoon. A passing ship was contacted and provided an exact position-fix which set his mind at ease. Only 50 miles to the next port and the prospect of a full night's sleep. *Poitín* crawled through the morning hours and by lunch time he estimated they were approaching the navigation lanes which separated the north- and south-bound ships. An uncomfortable lack of shipping stirred a nervous appetite which forced him below to forage through crackers and cheese. A fourth cup of coffee was not what he needed but the craving for caffeine had to be satisfied.

Anyway, a fourth coffee was nothing compared to the twelve or more needed to get him through a day's work in Sydney. It was nearly six years later when a friend explained how the major events in his life were a direct result of his own behaviour, something which helped him understand why he had left Australia. 'The subconscious,' or spirit, as Les preferred to call it, 'demands to experience life. It somehow knows what is lacking in a person's soul and seeks out the lessons necessary to help that person learn. Nothing too fancy, just a simple process of becoming a better person through the school of hard knocks. Any refusal to learn from a lesson and move on usually results in a shake up of daily life. It's often fear of the unknown which holds people back and causes them to become stuck in some form of destructive behaviour. Like a master beating a student for not carrying out his wishes, our inner spirit

can induce physical discomfort to help wake us to a higher purpose in life.'

For Dermot the potential to self-destruct was great. The
road ahead, as viewed from the tenth floor of a Sydney office
block, was paved with success but uninviting to the soul. And
so his deeper unrest commenced the process of disrupting
everyday life until the road became unbearable.

The caffeine, the alcohol and the drugs helped him fight
the humiliating world of panic attacks – a disturbing process
which sent him fleeing from social situations, frightened, confused and invariably gasping for breath. Always the same
question, 'why have you done this to yourself?' Always the
same feeling of shame, of having let himself down. The
destruction undermined his performance at work and he
found he was avoiding certain situations. At the time all
appeared to be in chaos but unknown to him it was organised
chaos, which helped make the decisions necessary to fulfil a
major goal later in life.

The humiliation could have been avoided had he taken the
time to examine his life and identify what he most wanted. He
had dismissed a single-handed ocean crossing as a boyhood
dream and buried himself in work for the sole purpose of prov-
ing he was as good as 'the other kids'.

'Life is a journey where someone else packs your luggage',
was how Les had helped explain things. 'Parental fears passed
down to children, in the hope of protecting them from hurtful
experiences, serve only to make them fearful.'

Dermot had collected childhood luggage which he had
aired so often it had multiplied in the re-packing – a process he
was not aware of but one which heavily influenced his adult
world. This personal luggage would have to be dumped in a
solitary ocean before he would be free to move ahead. He was
reluctant to encompass change and so he was dragged, by a
hungry spirit, through a confusing and painful period.

A blink of the eye beamed him back into the boat just as his mind was about to cross the Sydney Harbour Bridge. He tossed the lukewarm coffee over the side and checked the horizon for ships.

Through the summer haze he sighted what resembled a dark patch of land. A lack of sleep and the heat of the afternoon sun concocted a drowsiness, and he questioned what he saw. A quick re-working of the navigation confirmed *Poitín's* position; Ouessant was at least 25 miles away which placed it well out of view. Minutes spent staring at the distant haze revealed a black and white structure emerging from a smoke-filled cloud like a chubby waiter in a busy café. A ship dressed in traditional uniform, with five-storey accommodation block and steering bridge perched on top, moved steadly on a shimmering sea. Gradually, window specks appeared as stains on a formal white shirt and a breaking bow-wave revealed untucked shirt below black cummerbund.

A sudden transformation from distant waiter to lurching ship caught him by surprise. The floating mass of steel moulded itself into a super tanker whose enormous black hull, most of which lay below the surface, forced its way through the water in an uncertain direction. Tentative moments hung motionless, becalmed in his mind, as the ship veered to starboard and gradually made its way up the English Channel.

Sighting the ship confirmed that *Poitín* was approaching the Traffic Separation Zones off the coast of Ouessant. Soon a constant stream of vessels could be seen charging from the haze, each one displacing 100,000 tons or more. Like waiters shuffling from an unseen source, fat and cumbersome, with trays laden, they followed in one another's footsteps – bulky figures, with the manoeuvrability of shoe leather on wet marble, required miles in which to stop.

Unlike any other mode of transport known to man, maritime architecture had decided the driver was better located several hundred feet from the front; an obvious advantage in a head-on collision but it created an enormous blind spot under the bow.

For a vessel, fully laden with hundreds of containers stacked high on deck, anything within half a mile was lost from sight. He felt very much the midget on the giant café floor.

Without the wind to fill her sails, Dermot was at the mercy of *Poitín*'s little engine. Exact timing on his part was needed to find a way through. He eased closer to what he imagined was the edge of the maritime passageway and waited. Some ships passed closer than others and some appeared to move a little faster. He watched, anxiously timing their movements, calculating the distance between stern and bow, hoping to slip through the pacing fleet. Behind an enormous container ship, an opportunity emerged from the haze, being chased by a following hulk, a gap between heel and toe. He eyed the opportunity to the rhythm of *Poitín*'s engine.

Heel and toe, heel and toe, heel and toe! The time was right. *Poitín* scurried towards the opening with all twelve horses sucking diesel to their limit. The approaching ship appeared to move faster than the others, faster than he had estimated. For five nervous minutes he persisted until the situation began to look precarious. A horn growled an angry warning that reverberated across the water. He spun *Poitín* around without hesitation and motored at full gallop until the ship had passed.

Dermot decided to wait until the tailback of ships had cleared but each time a gap appeared another ship followed directly behind, and then another and another – all equally as big, all dangerous and menacing.

Half an hour passed without the slightest change in the procession. He began to realise that waiting would not create an opportunity or change the pattern of things. It would probably be just as busy at night and he had no intention of attempting to cross in the dark. The reality of the situation demanded he take a chance if he wanted to move forward.

Once more he eased *Poitín* towards the stream of ships. His mouth was dry, fear having a mighty thirst. The pounding of his heart filled his ears with a crazed rhythm. If only he had someone else on board to take bearings and offer an opinion on the best moment to make the break.

Another opening presented itself and without hesitation he drove *Poitín* at full speed on what was surely a collision course with the advancing ship. They converged, bow to bow, then bow to side and finally bow to open water. The ship passed. *Poitín* was at last heading for the gap which followed behind but in so doing moved into the path of the ensuing ship. 'Perfect timing,' he thought, 'just like I planned.' Then the engine seemed to slow as *Poitín* struggled through the turbulent wake left by the passing ship. He looked to the approaching hulk, imagined it to alter course and that *Poitín* had not yet moved across its bow. Too late to turn back, he felt a rising sensation of helplessness.

'I've got it wrong. I'm not going to make it ... oh Jaysus ...'

Time stopped. He stood watching the steel wall grow bigger as it bore down on him. Desperate to escape the advancing danger his body surged forward in a coaxing movement as if riding a stubborn mule. With each movement came the hope of nudging ahead. What was at first a conscious rhythm soon deteriorated into a mindless rocking – a rocking so familiar to jaded minds, eager for the comfort of some other place, like an infant on a mother's lap exhausted by the newness of it all, or a simpleton on a front porch wearied by the prospect of no escape. *Poitín* refused to be distracted by the mix of emotions and slowly, very slowly, the opposite side of the steel wall came into view.

An enormous sigh echoed from the depths of his lungs and he slid from the rocking horse onto the cockpit seat. Relief rushed over him. To his disappointment, he realised that neither engine nor ship had changed, his mind had simply exaggerated the danger. 'You windy bastard,' he chided 'there was stacks of room.'

Clearing the north-bound shipping lane was only half the job completed. There remained the south-bound lane. At least he could relax while he crossed the four-mile wide separation zone.

Plenty of time for a cup of tea before the next jig-a-jig with the mighty waiters. On a snippet of wind and the motor on half throttle, it was not long before the south-bound ships came into view; it seemed quieter with only a few ships in sight. 'Maybe this will be easier,' he thought.

'Oh shite,' he shouted as a thick cloud descended around him. 'No, not fog, not in the busiest shipping lane in the world ...' Within minutes his vision was reduced to the length of the boat. In the world of fat men on café floors, someone had just turned out the lights.

He checked the navigation and noted *Poitín*'s position in the middle of the separation zone. Until the fog lifted the only course of action was to stop the engine and wait. He finished making the cup of tea which the fog had interrupted and considered his options.

'Option one,' he thought, 'nothing happens, the ships see *Poitín* on their radar and manage to steer clear. Two, I get run down and succeed in getting into the dinghy and someone picks me up later. Three, I get run down, full stop, end of story.'

He knew the chances of surviving a collision were near to zero but he needed to feel he had some control in a helpless situation. 'Concentrate on option one,' he told himself. 'Be positive, you'll be okay.' He untied the dinghy which was lashed on deck and brought the 'panic bag' up from below. The bag contained flares, water, survival suit and food, all that he would require if he had to abandon the boat. *Poitín* was fitted with an excellent radar reflector, but he decided to wet the flapping sails which also helped to bounce the radar.

Sitting outside in the changing greyness played havoc with eyes already deprived of sleep. An hour passed and the fog refused to budge. The ships continued to pass in the distance using only artificial vision. He went below and tried to nap but the sound of engines and propellors filled his world. A deep-bellied rumbling droned through the heavy air and down the companionway. *Poitín*'s hull, like an enormous speaker, picked

58

up every underwater sound as if researching the mating call of an enormous sea creature.

Once *Poitín* remained in the dividing strip she was reasonably safe but there was no way of telling for how long that might last. He had to consider the tide flowing in one direction, any possible alteration in course by the ships and the direction of *Poitín*'s movement across the surface. The safest course of action was to wait and hope the fog lifted before nightfall.

Eventually a breeze arrived, like a new broom, and swept all before it. The evening sun was dusted off and distant ships were suddenly uncovered. The restoration of visibility and the power in the sails lifted his spirits. He tweaked the jib-sheet to extract the last ounce of speed and took delight in feeling *Poitín* slip through the water once again. The second shipping channel was like a country lane compared to the first experience. He felt far more confident under sail power and slipped through the passing ships without too much bother.

Ouessant appeared above the horizon as if expecting a late arrival. *Poitín* sailed well in the light air but 'ten miles' translated into time meant 'two hours'. He looked on helplessly, as piece by piece, the distant island was pilfered by the darkness which prowled from the east. A periodic light flashed a point-of-entry, like curtains flapping in an open window at the scene of the crime.

He took a bearing from the lighthouse and continued for another hour before dropping all sail and waiting for morning. The prospect of another night at sea, of random sleep, of keeping watch and checking position, increased the temptation to chance entering the rocky bay. The promise he made at Land's End stuck in his mind like a chicken bone, threatening to choke what good luck remained.

Too tired to sleep, he made a cup of coffee and sat outside in the fresh night air. It had been an eventful day but he had come through unscathed. In fact, he felt happy with how he had coped. His first encounter with a supertanker was no more testing than his first sprint across the bow of an Irish trawler – it was simply bigger.

By midnight he was stupefied by the lack of sleep over the previous two days. He tried to cat nap, but each time disturbing dreams clamoured through his mind. He eventually questioned whether there was something evil on board and sought childhood comfort in turning on the light. Relieved there was no one to witness this juvenile action he forced himself out of the warm sleeping bag and put the kettle on. He remembered a single-handed sailor warning that his mind would play games when it became extremely tired and would require serious effort to control the menacing thoughts. He calculated the tidal currents for the next four hours and went below once again to sleep. Regardless of how he tried, sleep was not to be had. 'Only two hours more before making our way into port,' he thought.

The summer night was soon chased off by another long June day and by 07:00 *Poitín* was safely tied to a mooring buoy in Lampaul Bay. He made a cup of tea and wrote up his diary:

1 JUNE
Entered with leading light bearing 060°. I felt I was sailing into the jaws of an enormous animal. If the devil were a marine creature he would look like this place. What an ugly entrance. Horrible feeling. Very tired, my mind is playing games. Get a grip.

Believe all the Lies you Hear

'Café aux lait' was not how it sounded.

'... ehh ... coffee con ... no, em ... cafeee con leje, si vout plait,' said with a jaded slur, did not prompt the French barman into action.

Dermot's third day without sleep. Unwashed, unshaven, and an unintelligible mix of schoolboy French and Linguaphone Spanish put him in the running for the title of town drunk. A request for alcohol would certainly have seen him tossed out on the street. The only course of action it seemed was to keep his mouth closed and point to the expresso machine.

A negative wave of his finger refused the barman's suggestion of a small cup. A positive nod of the head agreed to a bigger one, a negative finger once again to a large black coffee and finally, a nodding acceptance of a coffee with lots of hot milk.

Some final complication then halted delivery to the client – the barman was being difficult, and enjoying it. Dermot's outstretched arm politely relieved him of the steaming delight. 'Just give me the shaggin' coffee' was barely hidden behind an exaggerated smile. He felt belligerent, even prickly, but his upbringing as a hotel proprietor's son had instilled an acceptance that the client was always right. Too tired to notice he was on the receiving side, he laid a handful of holiday coins on the counter and gave the barman the opportunity to play the finger game.

He sat at a window-table, mindless of the transformation

which spiralled in the cup below – pure white froth sinking in the rich brown flow. Such a spectacle so often used to pass away the time but was now lost to a vacant stare. The unique ambience of black tobacco, fresh coffee and Gallic chat yanked his nose as it escaped through the open window. He couldn't help but look across the bay.

The 'ugly marine creature' from the night before was now a fresh young girl enjoying a beautiful summer's morning. The high ground to the far side of the bay was dressed in a lush green skirt with rock-black tights, water marked up to the knees, as if just having stepped ashore. Lampaul, her only jewel, had terraced houses which hung like strings of pearls above the bay. The tide had ebbed from the tiny harbour, leaving small inshore fishing boats resting their bottoms on the glistening sand.

Poitín very nearly slipped his eye as she lay quietly anchored below. He could not remember coming ashore but was glad to be off the boat. He really felt like talking to someone. However, his lack of French appeared to rule that out. The past few days had been spent alone, in the silent confines of the boat, and now that he was among people he felt more alone than ever before.

The television at the end of the bar offered some relief; lots of colour and plenty of beautiful people, perfect for keeping a stupefied mind entertained. His eyes slowly closed and for a few seconds he watched the TV images which followed him into sleep. A few adjoining seconds of bliss quickly passed, until somewhere deep inside his skull a balance mechanism tripped. His neck responded in a startled move which jerked his head upright; eyes flashed open, surprised by the sudden action. Feeling conspicuous, he looked around the bar, yet nothing had changed. The expresso machine hissed steam into a bottomless jug of milk, while people chatted and continued to fill the air with smoke. The flashing screen whizzed one frantic commercial after another, forcing him to turn away. *Poitín* looked up from the calm of the bay and his bed whispered his name.

That night he dreamt there were crew on board who kept watch while he slept. Believing they had abandoned *Poitín* and left her drifting towards the rocks, he woke and jumped out into the cockpit. Though he could see the shore in the distance and the cold night air chilled his face, he still felt in danger. After some time the dream subsided and he accepted the reality of the situation; *Poitín* was safely anchored for the night. He checked the mooring line before going back to bed. The warning system which helped him to stay awake at sea was working on over drive.

***

The next morning he had a late breakfast and decided to wait on board for the lunchtime weather forecast. Before heading out into the Bay of Biscay, he needed to see the synoptic chart on TV, or better still, get a long-range weather forecast from the Met office.

While he lounged about the boat, another Irishman was busy buying fresh bread in the village. 'Ah John, there is a boat from your country in the bay, arrived last night. The first for some time, yes?'

Seán, known to the locals as John, was always warmly received. He was after all an 'Atlantic islander' and he shared a love affair with a local girl.

As Dermot doodled over a chart of Biscay, a dinghy came alongside and pressed up against *Poitín*, causing her to rock gently. He could not believe his ears when he heard someone call out, '*Poitín*, anyone on board'. He rushed out on deck nearly tripping over his own, 'Hello, how are you? I'm Dermot, come on board'.

John made arrangements with the driver of the dinghy to pick him up later in the afternoon, while Dermot slipped below to hastily make room for his welcome guest.

He was eager for conversation and John hungered for the familiarity of home. They quickly embarked on a process of

63

exploration, hoping to establish a mutual bond. A friendly interrogation commenced, eager to reveal where their paths might have crossed. John had been to County Wicklow, which was close enough for Dermot to rattle off a few familiar names and paint descriptions which they could both share.

And so the afternoon began and continued. They searched through past schools, colleges and friends, in the hope of deeper ties. Eventually they moved on to Lampaul, to what had brought them there and the desires and expectations which had launched them on their separate ways. A simple and honest exercise, gingerly undertaken in everyday life but hurried by passing travellers for whom time is at a premium – a natural reaction to human insecurity which needed to be overcome through mirrored beliefs, likes and dislikes, people and places. Safety in numbers, even for those who appeared to go their own way, gave a welcome opportunity to relax and recharge the batteries which powered that very individuality. They moved out into the cockpit to enjoy the afternoon sun but really it was to instigate a change of tempo. Like old friends, they settled into a more relaxed conversation which rose and fell like long rolling waves with silences surfing between the crests.

Three years previously, on a two week holiday, Isabelle had made her way to the Aran Islands and met John. 'It was almost as if I was waiting for her, maybe I was. I'm not too sure about this sort of thing. Anyway, I followed her back to Lampaul and I've been here ever since.' He had passed three of the happiest years of his life on this desolate outpost off the French coast and had no plans to move.

Dermot tried as best he could to explain the driving force behind his sailing alone, but as always he resorted to describing the challenge of the Atlantic. How was he to explain a deep need to break through the surface and expose hidden emotion? – an exorcism which might advance him or leave scars so deep as to render him unrecognisable to himself. John very kindly accepted the chatter about the challenge of the Atlantic but suspected something was being held back. The whine of the dinghy returned, like an annoying fly, to interrupt the discussion but they agreed to continue later in the evening.

Dermot's orange-coloured inflatable stood out among the local craft as it entered the half-full harbour. He pulled the dinghy above the short marine weed which continued to drain long after the tide had left it lying limp on the paving stones. A grand metal ring with layers of rusty bark, chipped and broken, hung from a stone wall.

John and Isabelle lived in an old stone house which, like so many on the island, had been divided to help hide the emptiness left by a dwindling population. They were fortunate to occupy the south-facing part to the back which looked out over the bay and any available sunsets.

Isabelle was not quite beautiful but blessed with a combination of attractive features that left the observer confused as to what was missing. Dermot tried not to stare while she moved about the kitchen, tight blue jeans, white cotton blouse and shoulder-length hair tied to reveal her slender neck. Like sun reflected from afar, her sex appeal flashed with certain movements – movements which twisted and curved, defining her character with the uniqueness of a glistening sea.

Crab mornay was what she had prepared for supper and in the journey, from cold bucket to boiling pan, the crabs seemed to nip a little of that feminine French touch. Her hand lunged into the bucket of waiting pincers with the expertise of a fishmonger's daughter, sending a nervous shiver through Dermot.

They suppered by the half-open window, talked, enjoyed good wine and watched the evening sun project a burning horizon onto the kitchen wall. Jokes were followed by laughter. Dermot flirted a little with Isabelle which pleased her in an embarrassed sort of way. John accepted this behaviour as a vote of confidence in his choice of partner, more an act of male camaraderie than any sexual proposition. Sillier by the hour, the fun increased until John suggested they go to the local pub.

Dermot could see they were a popular couple in the village. John was in his element, taunting and teasing the local fishermen. Dermot was introduced as 'a real sailor', which embarrassed him somewhat, especially when he thought of *Poitín*'s exploits. Without a knowledge of the language there was nothing he could do except to refute John's exaggerated statements.

After a few cold beers, the lack of sleep over the past few days and the excitement of the voyage all hit him at once. He felt ready to collapse and John insisted he stay at their place for the night. Isabelle agreed and promised to call him early the next morning.

He drifted towards sleep thinking about *Poitín* securely anchored in the bay and imagined Isabelle safely tucked up in bed. Thoughts of beautiful women past, of scented hair, misty skin, determined giving and generous taking, led him to a place far from the sea. He dreamt of lushness, undulating countryside and beauty.

... a young girl lies in a field. Flowers strain to see. Innocence to innocence. A summer breeze rushes through the trees, warm air on hot skin, the hand of nature touches her without intrusion. Overcome with joy, she rolls to face the sun. Beauty shines on beauty, soft skin on warm grass, again a touch is sneaked.

The valley rejoices, for she is the reflection of itself, to be indulged and taken into its heart. A large oak laughs through whiskered moss on aged bark. A young fir rolls its head and yelps so loud the sun casts a ray upon its face. A celebration dance. Roots tap to the rhythm of the young girl's heart. Trunks sway to the chorus of an aviary choir. Dizzy fun without restraint, pure, divine, a pulse beyond the norm. A heart of fun exhilarates the world. A pitch is reached that cannot be ignored.

***

Around the time when fishermen step quietly from the night to set about their daily work, *Poitín* cast off the mooring buoy and began to make her way across Lampaul Bay. As slumber breath clouds a bedroom window, a morning mist obscured the lower shore. Being present to watch the night pull bedcovers from the sleeping day was his special joy. He loved the slow awakening; a unique time when all is at peace with itself, without conjured dreams or daily fears. A time free of thought, past or future.

With 350 miles of open water across the Bay of Biscay to La Coruña in the north of Spain his mind set to work. Imagined anxiety might have distracted him had it not been for the persistent Atlantic swell breaking itself upon the rocky jaws up ahead. There was a light north-west wind and *Poitín* made four knots under engine and mainsail. As he approached the rocks at the mouth of the bay, the wind freshened slightly, prompting him to hoist the headsail. After years of sailing, he still managed to hoist the number four without the tack properly attached and up went the sail to the top of the mast. *Poitín* shuddered as if suddenly aware of the jaws and the strong tide which carried saliva-like streaks across the bay. With little room for error, he rushed forward and tugged on the sail, to no avail.

With the headsail flapping mischievously at the top of the mast, he turned *Poitín* and motor-sailed back towards Lampaul. Under the shelter of the cliff shore the sail seemed to lose interest and willingly slid onto the deck. 'You bastard, why couldn't you do that a few minutes ago?' Also cursing himself for making such a basic mistake, he double-checked the sails and prepared to get under way once again.

By 09:00 he was steering 210^0 magnetic with a nice, fresh breeze and an ebb tide pushing him along. He had not managed to see a synoptic weather chart but the short-range weather forecast from the BBC was favourable. A discussion with the sea captain who helped him understand celestial navigation slipped into his mind. When he had asked what 'Biscay' was really like, Danny thought for a moment and then replied, 'Well, you can believe all the lies you hear about it.' 'Christ, Danny, that's all I need to hear.'

'Listen Dermot, if we get into trouble in an ocean-going ship we have to rely on life-rafts the size of *Poitín*. A large vessel poses an obstruction to the waves whereas your little boat will bop around like a cork.'

He told himself to settle down and look after his boat. Why was he worrying about talk of 'Biscay' when he was enjoying a sail in good, fresh conditions. Isabelle had packed fresh crab-meat from the night before and gave it to him before leaving. John had also offered a bottle of table wine, 'should the weather get a bit rough'.

They were a lovely couple who had found something special in their lives and he felt a little of it rubbed off on the people they met. They had what he regarded as the perfect relationship. They were good friends who respected each other and had regard for the other's opinion, but underneath they showed signs of love and affection.

Dermot's relationships never seemed to make it to that level of maturity. They started well: passionate, attentive and over-loving, which invariably lulled honest hearts into a false sense of security. He tried to take love, never realising that love can only be given. His need to quickly find a special place in a girl's heart usually ended in panic when faced with the consequences of his behaviour.

His most recent experience had hinted at a more mature approach. Maybe it was her young age that had forced him to finally show some responsibility for his actions. She had been warned to expect the worst and told him so – all that remained was for him to prove her right. He held the power to create something beautiful between them, or shatter her budding emotions. Her heart, like a newly-formed crystal glass, ready for love's rich wine, was lifted from the blower's shelf by one of life's accomplished cutters.

Jane was young and beautiful, her head in the clouds, yet no more than was respectable for her years. They shared a special time together, both growing and learning despite the decade and a half between them. Female intuition helped her sense his fear for her and she tried bravely to conceal her increasing emotions. He could feel they were growing ever closer but he was as ready to form a lasting relationship as the day he first kissed a girl. Like an early warning shot fired across her bow, he shared his dream of sailing an ocean 'alone'.

The wind continued to increase all morning and by midday he had reduced sail to triple-reefed main and heavy weather jib. As the wind and seas grew, he questioned whether he should have opted for a plain cheese sandwich instead of Isabelle's rich crab salad. Even with reduced sail area, *Poitín* raced along at an exciting six knots with a two-metre swell on the starboard beam. He lacked the experience of ocean sailing to notice that the swell had arrived well before the wind; something had stirred up the ocean.

Without the sun's spotlight in which to perform, the wind lost enthusiasm and settled down for the evening. *Poitín* was treated to a little more sail area but was still underpowered. 'I can't risk being caught in the black of night with too much sail,' he thought. 'Better to take my time and relax for the evening.'

A number of fishing boats, probably trailing long nets, prowled the midnight sea. He watched their silent movements as they circled their prey. Dots of light; red, then white, then green. In his mind, imaginary shapes were constructed to fill the void between each set of lights and then manned by imaginary crew. He curled up under the canvas sprayhood and cat-napped while *Poitín* see-sawed her way over the increasing swell. The trawlers eventually ceased their movements and he imagined their nets as enormous paws scooping their kill into empty bellies. Like dogs sniffing their way across distant hills, they continued on their way and left *Poitín*, her masthead light as a lone star on the night sea.

The passing of the boats also left an opportunity for him to put his head down. He managed three hours of closed eyes and two of sleep before he woke feeling tired but rested. A quick sweep of the horizon revealed nothing to worry about in the way of shipping. Before preparing breakfast he slackened off the main sail to help the boat ride the lively motion that had built up overnight.

The long process of preparing food in fresh winds and a rolling sea began. First, the frying pan was removed from the safety of the locker and clamped to the gimballed cooker. Then the packet of bacon, while wedged between hand and work surface, was carefully cut open. He pressed himself against the edge of the panel which separated his bunk from the cooker and spread the bacon upon the dancing pan. Both hands were occupied when the boat lurched under a rogue wave, throwing him backwards across the cabin. He caught the protective bar in front of the cooker and walloped his hip as he was spun round onto the bunk.

He paused for a while, then reached across and lit the cooker. All that remained was to manoeuvre the eggs from the locker to the pan, find the bread, the butter, somehow spread one on the other and then ensure the finished product found its way directly into his mouth. It was only 06.30 and he had all the time he required. It was going to be a long day.

Due to the cloud cover he could not get a midday sight with the sextant and so decided to sail a little more westerly. Unlike the entrance to the English Channel there was no defined shipping lane across the Bay of Biscay but he knew that most ships followed a straight line between the north of Spain and the north of France. By altering course a few degrees to the west he would probably come upon a ship and could check his position.

Around supper time he sighted a ship in the distance which he called on the radio. 'Black merchant vessel, headed north by northeast, approximate position ... This is the sailing yacht two miles off your starboard bow ...' His call was eventually answered and gave a position of $46^0.07'$N, $07^0.04'$W, only two miles from where he had estimated. Once *Poitín*'s whereabouts were confirmed, he continued on his way, altering course slightly to avoid any ships by nightfall.

Overall he was enjoying himself and made the best of the

more-than-lively sailing conditions. At times he felt a twinge of loneliness but that was to be expected. Most importantly he felt comfortable with his handling of *Poitín*. Like cooking breakfast, all that was ever required was to take the time to work with the rhythm of the sea.

As the lunchtime potatoes burst into a boiling frenzy he lowered the gas and allocated time out to write up his diary:

> I'm developing an interesting relationship with *Poitín*. The driving force within that compelled me to do this trip seems to have occupied the boat and is now giving me the confidence and strength to continue. The same spirit seems to rest when I rest, but eventually gets itchy feet and orders me up on deck.

It was midnight when the BBC gave the weather forecast he had hoped he would not hear in Biscay '... gale warnings for Finesterre and Biscay, force six, seven and eight later'. One part of his mind taunted, 'now let's see what the great single-handed sailor is made of', while the other pleaded to be woken from a dreadful nightmare. 'I need more time to prepare for this kind of madness, I'm not ready yet.'

'You can believe all the lies you hear about it,' repeated again and again in his head, like a sacred mantra. Fragile courage dropped from his stomach leaving an empty pit. The void was quickly filled with a fear which percolated up his spine to his head.

Confused, he sat staring at the chart hoping someone would miraculously appear to get him out of this mess. The radio squeaked and screamed its way into the background noise of rushing water and wind. His thoughts escaped into a daydream; nature's sedative, to help calm a frantic mind and save it from itself.

He thought about the freak waves reported to form when Atlantic swells reached the relatively shallow tidal waters of the Continental Shelf. He tried but failed not to think about the ship from his home town which sank in Biscay only a few months previously. 'Jesus Christ, man. Pull yourself together, prepare, get the boat ready, prepare, come on.'

Twelve hours later his imaginings were put to the test and forced to stand alongside their reality. As the gale increased he changed to smaller sails, then reefed, and reefed again, until reduced to the minimum.

His thoughts went back to those sleepless nights when he walked the quay at home, trying to imagine himself alone at sea in gale conditions, changing sails in the black of night. Now he was actually doing it, without anyone to help and all was going well. It was his first real ocean gale and although he was scared the conditions were not quite as bad as he had imagined. He found the most comfortable place to sleep was on the floor of the cabin, wedged in with cushions. And that was how the next 24 hours passed.

At first he tried keeping a lookout but due to the poor visibility could only glimpse the surrounding sea when lifted high on the crest of a wave. *Poitín* handled the gale superbly, but every so often a big wave broke across her decks with a deafening noise, knocking her off course as if rammed by a passing ship. Each time she shuddered and rolled over on her side for what seemed like an eternity before coming upright and continuing on her way. Most of the day he spent listening to the radio, trying not to think about what was happening outside.

Dermot slept little that night with the noise of the breaking seas crashing about him and the violent motion of the boat. He took some comfort in the fact that *Poitín* was at last in deep water, away from the Continental Shelf and the real threat. Once he slowed the boat down and gave her a chance to cope with the waves, conditions onboard became less difficult and marginally comfortable. The biggest worry was not the weather being experienced but what he imagined was yet to come.

The following morning the weather forecast was for another day of force seven and eight from the west, which offered a repeat of the previous 24 hours. He was encouraged by *Poitín*'s performance and how he had coped. As the day wore on he became increasingly aggressive, annoyed for having allowed his imagination to run wild. He felt a growing desire to push the boat to her limit. Steering southwest with all the sails sheeted in hard, *Poitín* punched her way through the seas. Spray broke across the boat, drenching him whenever he left the shelter of the cockpit. The water invariably found its way inside his wet-weather gear, soaking him to the skin, increasing his anger.

Tired and bruised from the endless motion of the boat as the gale raged into its second day, he felt his enthusiasm wane. There was nowhere to hide, no room with closed door. He inhaled saturated air into his lungs through a mouth which tasted only of sea. Evaporated spray left salt caked on dry skin, and the incessant wind throbbed noisily inside his head. He was in the gale and the gale in him.

He hated having to leave the safety of the cockpit to crawl aft and lean out over the stern to adjust the self-steering but deep down he experienced the most amazing sense of excitement. This excitement, together with the danger and the feeling of speed, as *Poitín* charged through the water, were both intoxicating and exhausting. The constant whine of the wind through the rigging and the noise of the breaking water added to the madness and the thrill.

The sun broke through a gap in the clouds that scurried across an industrial-like sky. The whole situation became surreal. Spray formed brilliant rainbows suspended in sunlight. Dazzling creations, like Namaqua flowers, were short-lived, for the wind drove them into the sea with a force that showed little regard for beauty. For a time he felt he had encountered two winds: one creative and friendly, one dangerously destructive. *Poitín* screamed through the water, creating her own rainbows as the spray flew across the decks. There was an amazing combination of violence, power and beauty, never before experienced by him. Unlike human violence, there was no sense of evil. Instead, it verged on an extreme form of aggressive playfulness.

He found himself immersed in a world of frenzied confusion that was oblivious to his presence.

When the self-steering veered off course, he roared in anger. He paused to consider what was happening. It was his first real excursion towards the edge, and he found it petrifying and intoxicating: a madness-cocktail blended from fatigue, fear, and excitement.

He remembered long-forgotten schoolboy lines from the mad King Lear, 'Blow, winds, and crack your cheeks! Rage! Blow!'

'Yeah, blow all you want, you bastard ... I don't care, blow you cataracts and hurricanes ... piss off!'

He climbed into the chaos of the cabin and began the laborious task of making a cup of soup. Before he could wedge himself into a comfortable position, the boat heaved and he watched helplessly as tomato soup raced across the chart and haemorrhaged onto the floor. Cursed out, increasingly indifferent, he sat staring at the mess. A thought lapped on his mind, a smile trickled down his face, washed over salted eyes and settled on parched lips. He remembered the fisherman in Rosslare and wondered what he would think of it all. 'Why would you want to make it any harder than it already is?'

The Early Light

Dermot felt the shelter from the north coast of Spain long before it came into view. As they sailed into calmer seas *Poitín* began to make real progress and he chanced changing into the last dry clothes.

Throughout the afternoon the distant land rose progressively above the horizon until cliff tops lined the sky. In a token act of defiance he unclipped the umbilical cord to his harness and stepped from the safety of the cockpit. Perched on the aft rail, as if resting from a long migration, he contemplated the surroundings with new eyes. His physical exhaustion could not curtail the rekindled sense of invincibility. If ever he could have accepted death it would have been in the thick of that gale. He could have gone with defiance and courage; could have grasped death by the throat, rather than wait to be taken, old, uncertain and afraid; could have rampaged through hell and charged his way into heaven. He had been goaded by the elements and experienced the power to confront God.

Poitín had behaved like never before, as had he. And now the rolling swell, the gentle wind, stroked the sails in a calming movement as if preparing him for human contact once more. His navigation was down to guesswork and Estaca de Bares seemed the most likely name for the estuary up ahead. There were no guarantees that what lay under the surface corresponded to the detail on the chart, but it felt right.

Dermot eased *Poitín* up the estuary, watching the depth sounder in the hope of identifying contour lines on the chart. The high cliff shore on either side barred entry to the south-west wind and rolling sea. The gale was not welcome here. He found the new calm unsettling, more so for having spent the last two days forcing himself to accept the wild conditions. He eyed the sky with suspicion and checked over his shoulder, half expecting a rogue wave to come screaming from the madhouse of Biscay, dishevelled, spray flying from its crest, stumbling over the rocky shore as it pursued him one last time.

He passed a town to the left but decided to keep going; a series of buoys marked a channel leading further inland. Having rounded a cliff to starboard a small harbour jammed with fishing boats of all sizes came into view. A small village clung precariously to the side of the cliff as if centuries before it had been wrecked there in a mighty flood. Loose terracotta-tiled roofs perched on blue-white walls had somehow found a foothold where none seemed possible.

Tucked away in the shelter of the surrounding mountains, there was no sign of the gale that continued to rage in the open sea. He was excited at the prospect of tying *Poitín* up safely for the night and going ashore. As if eager to rest, *Poitín* slipped into an empty berth with only the hint of a touch on the tiller.

Once the cabin was tidied and the chaos of the past two days removed, he made his way to the only café by the harbour. Heads turned when he first entered. Fishermen, unaccustomed to foreigners, protected their patch with defiant looks. Safe in the aura of the pack they glanced, confident and indifferent, at the intruder. When he enquired about clearing customs he was told that the nearest port of entry was La Coruña. The barman agreed to phone the local police and explain that *Poitín* had arrived in Estaca de Bares and was sheltering from the gale. At first it appeared the police might come and check him out, until he explained he was alone. They would note his arrival and suggested he clear customs when in La Coruña. It seemed that local crime was not perpetrated by individuals in small boats.

Once he had the all-clear from the police, Dermot relaxed and enjoyed a cold beer before phoning home. Previous calls had been overshadowed by the imminent crossing of Biscay. The memory of his parents looking sad and confused on the morning of his departure nudged a pang of guilt to the fore. The emotions he extracted from them on that occasion were about to be returned, with interest. He knew the sound of his voice, alive and well, would lift them from their pit of worried imaginings. The pride of having crossed Biscay alone was his gift to them, a winning rosette to be worn on the owner's lapel. He felt his heart lurch at the thought of their joy, his father's congratulations, their concern, his mother's declaration of love. His eyes flooded at the thought of his father's voice struggling with unspoken emotion.

The vino tinto helped him sleep through the first wave of early morning activity. A few knocks on *Poitín*'s hull from someone's weathered knuckles soon had him up on deck. A half-smile and glance at *Poitín*'s stern line from the man with the knuckles said all that was needed; Dermot cast-off the small fishing boat.

Before the harbour had completely emptied he walked to the bar and enquired who could service the alternator. The café owner quickly interrupted and advised that a cousin of his could taxi Dermot around the estuary to a motor repair shop, suggesting it was too dangerous to cross the estuary by boat. Dermot knew the bar owner was lining him up for a rip-off, as he had done the night before with the price of a shower and meal, so in his best broken Spanish he explained that he had arrived by boat and would leave by boat, 'y no necisito un taxi'.

A teenage boy working on the quay took time from repairing lobster pots to describe the safest route to Ortigueira. The boy helped to cast off the lines and smiled as *Poitín* moved from the quay. Dermot made his way across the tree-lined bay without any problem to the town he had spotted the previous day. He realised it was his fear of the gale which caused him to go so far inland.

After another good night's sleep he began to feel more human and was eager to get sailing. Ortigueira proved to be a friendly place, or at least that's how it seemed after his brief visit ashore, it's only drawback being that the alternator repair man was on holiday. By 08:00 the following morning, *Poitín* was making her way across the bay, headed for the open sea. An early morning fisherman returning to port indicated the way was clear of any dangers and to continue straight out. 'Muchas gracias', 'Adios', passed between them as they both waved and went their separate ways.

The sail around Cape Ortegal to La Coruña was an absolute joy. With a glorious blue sky and a force five north-east wind, *Poitín* skipped along as if Biscay had never been crossed. A few ships passed nearby but he felt sure they would have someone on watch being that close in to shore. He called a ship which was headed in his direction to check that they had seen *Poitín*, and was answered by a male voice from Liverpool. Dermot explained the alternator was out of action and that without sufficient battery power he could not transmit for very long. The Liverpudlian seemed happy to talk unanswered, passing away the boredom of his watch. His recollections of Dublin back in 1965 when he was last there kept Dermot amused. Pubs which had since changed name, ballrooms which no longer existed and girls who had ceased roaming the quays, painted memories of a city any forlorn sailor would enjoy preserving. Dermot recognised the loneliness in the voice yet there was a calmness which suggested that loneliness was now a familiar bed-mate.

Later in the afternoon he sighted La Coruña, the Spanish gateway to the North Atlantic and his original destination before being blown off course. The very name smacked of serious seamanship, of the Atlantic, of achievement. He felt eager to dock in the shadow of the 'Hercules' light and impatiently nudged *Poitín* up the Ria de la Coruña.

Dinghies trickled out of the harbour for the twilight races.

Like signets learning to swim they followed in an obedient line behind the committee boat which led the way to the far side of the bay. The clubhouse at the marina was new and uninviting but to his surprise the bar buzzed with yachties of all nationalities. While waiting at the counter he struck up a conversation with the crew of a British yacht on their way to Mallorca. They seemed eager for fresh input to the conversation and before long he was swapping jokes and telling stories of bad weather and big waves.

A French single-handed sailor who had just arrived from Tristan da Cuñha in the South Atlantic joined the group. He had stopped off in La Coruña on his way home to repair a broken rudder. When he discovered Dermot was starting out on his first solo voyage he took him under his wing. Jacques had passed the last 42 days alone at sea. 'Mon ami, somsing very impotent,' he said. 'Ju most alweys eet. No mat-teer ohw tsired ju fil, ju most eet, otser-wise you luse tse en-urgee tu pri-par jur food and tsen ju will diee.'

'Aah Jacques, are you seriously trying to tell me that aside from being run down by a passing ship, swamped by an enormous wave, sinking, falling overboard, or even solitary madness, that the biggest danger of single-handed sailing is malnutrition?' The group erupted into laughter and the unfortunate Frenchman was lost under a barrage of banter.

'You French and your love affair with food, it doesn't have to be cordon bleu for me. Baked beans straight from the can will do.'

Jacques' attempt to qualify his statement stood little chance of being heard, and he resorted to outlandish insults on English cooking.

Of all the people Dermot encountered in La Coruña it was the skipper of a small Australian boat who made a lasting impression. Benny and Dermot quickly touched a common chord, not on any particular subject, but more of an understanding on how life should feel. They downed a few cold beers on a street terrace in the old part of town and traded stories of their past and expectations for the future.

Dermot described his experience on the night he waited to enter Lampaul, when the growing tiredness had begun to play games with his mind. As the memory returned he was dismayed at how a simple and straightforward situation had become so precarious. He had been warned that it was common for people sailing alone to have that sort of experience but he was surprised by the sense of evil.

'One theory is that both good and evil co-exist all around us, like television channels,' said Benny. 'Good operates on a higher frequency than evil ... if your mind becomes exhausted as in your case, it exposes your spirit to lower frequencies, somewhere between bad and evil. It sounds to me like you glimpsed the wrong channel before shaking yourself out of it.' Benny pushed his chair away from the table. 'Does that make any sense ... or does it sound like a load of crap?' Rising to his feet, he continued, 'Don't say anything for the moment. Think about it, while I get the drinks.'

There was certainly nothing complicated in what Benny had said. It was just new, different, and Dermot was eager to know more. Alcohol, the great liberator, made quicksand of Dermot's established beliefs. Before Benny had slid the beers across the table Dermot asked, 'where did you learn about this stuff?' Benny thought for a second, remembering the first time he had asked the very same question. He had been overly excited by the snippets which he received but at the time felt certain he had found a living guru who could answer any questions about life and help map out the future.

'The basis of what I know I picked up in books but the cementing of the lessons came in everyday life. I wasted a lot of time trying to make a master of a very fine person who was simply further down the same road as myself. He had the good sense to allow me to stumble over my own desire for an infallible guru but was sensitive enough to catch me before I fell. He knew that the humiliation of such a fall would have sent me running from anything further to do with such open thinking.

'In the world of new thinking and spirituality people are no different, they want the easiest and fastest way forward – "MacGuru and fries", so to speak.

'I'm sure there are special people in the world,' he continued, 'with highly-evolved intuition or psychic skills, but the reality is we are all a chip off the same Almighty Block. We all have something to teach each other, we're all part of a particular spiritual group.'

Dermot fingered the gold-coloured condensation which formed on the glass. 'You'll have to run that one past me again, what's a spiritual group?'

He listened while Benny explained his belief that a soul needed to experience many lives before it could reach the level of perfection needed to enter heaven, or as he preferred to call it 'become pure spirit'. 'So, the "Head Man" gathers our souls together into spiritual groups which then live out their lives on earth as families, friends, lovers, acquaintances, even enemies. But, each time, lifetime that is, they live different roles. That's why I said to take note of everyone around you, both good and bad. Not only those people close to you, but casual contacts as well. They are part of your group and have something to teach you on a spiritual level.'

'Jaysus, Benny. That's a bit heavy. Are you telling me that someone like that bar owner I met the other day, remember the one I told you about, who ripped me off, is part of my spiritual group? What did I learn from him?'

'Maybe,' said Benny, 'just maybe, he learned something from you, or at least had the opportunity to do so. Maybe the way you dismissed his little scam by refusing to squabble was meant to show it up as the waste of time it really was.

'Sometimes, Dermot, a parent has to reprimand a child in the short term to help it improve or learn something that is important later in life. The child might hate what is happening at the time, might even hate its parent, but later on, when the child has a greater understanding of how life works, it might appreciate the lesson behind the pain. The stronger the spirit, the harder the lesson.'

And so the evening went, drinking less and talking more until they were interrupted by the British crew and the Frenchman on their way back to the marina. Unable to persuade them to continue on their way, Dermot and Benny decided to join 'the team' for one last drink in the marina bar.

Jacques was blind drunk when he later said goodbye but once again, he mumbled advice to Dermot about making sure to eat. The fact that he was skin and bone made Dermot wonder at the time how close the Frenchman had come to dying. There was a disturbed look in Jacques' eyes, which Dermot would only recognise months later.

He enjoyed La Coruña and the people he met, especially Benny who was by far the most interesting. Much of what Benny had said was new to him but it all had the potential to make sense. All going well, they would run into each other again, further down the coast.

He departed La Coruña early, at a time before the tide or night had begun to ebb. It felt strange leaving the bright safety of the port behind to head out into the darkness. *Poitín*'s navigation lights cut a path through the blackness which filled the bay. Although he failed to get the alternator repaired in La Coruña, he did manage to have the batteries charged sufficiently to supply power for the voyage to Bayona.

Once clear of the harbour Dermot took solace in the familiarity of a cup of milky tea and a few wholegrain biscuits. A simple pleasure which could so easily go unnoticed in everyday life was once again a major comfort in the solitary existence he lived when at sea.

As the early light began to give form to his surroundings he decided it was safe to pass through a narrow channel to the west of the bay. In the distance rows of terraced lights began to take shape as an enormous passenger liner made her way into port. She was headed for the same short cut as *Poitín* and blew a deep-bellied horn at the tiny dot on her radar screen. 'I'mmmmm biggerrrr thaaan youuuu' seemed to bellow from the horn and warned the dot to step aside, 'oor eeeelse'. *Poitín* moved closer to the rocks, into shallow water and waited while the fat lady had the last say.

By 06:55 he was well under way and went below to listen to the BBC weather forecast. He wasn't too surprised to hear that the wind was to reach force seven around Cape Finisterre, where he was headed. The local forecast had predicted force five for open waters and he knew from experience that wind always accelerates around high headlands. Force seven was stronger that he would have liked, 'but at least it was blowing in the right direction,' he thought.

Rounding Cape Finisterre, with its choppy seas and strong wind, proved a lively event. Once around the Cape the sea conditions settled and he found himself in sheltered waters which rippled towards a beautiful sandy bay.

The day was all but spent by the time he found a suitable place to anchor for the night. He felt as though *Poitín* was being pursued by the very darkness she had chased into the arms of the morning sun. Lights began to flicker on boats anchored around the bay and laughter carried across the water as sundowners began to take affect. He felt safe in the company of other boats – bigger boats, which smacked of maturity, as if the bay was supervised by adults who knew what they were doing.

He set about preparing an evening meal of packet rice with tinned stew and waited outside while the little gas cooker did all within its power to resuscitate the bloated bag. Funny how he had failed to master cooking during the years in the hotel. Maybe he just never wanted to learn, afraid it was yet another knot in the imagined rope of woven excuses which tied him to the business and *Poitín* to the quay.

The summer nights were warmer now further south and he felt very much as if he was cruising in foreign waters. The coastline looked different, even at night, or so he thought and he began to savour the excitement of exploring new places.

***

The passage to Bayona was slow and hot. All day the sun beamed down and what little breeze there was died completely by midday. The bad weather which had kept him anchored in the shelter of Cape Finisterre for two days had wrung any enthusiasm from the wind.

When in La Coruña he had banged his knee while manoeuvring *Poitín* out of the berth. It had slowly grown to the size of a melon and he feared it might be something more than just a bad bruise. When changing sails on the foredeck, kneeling was impossible, which made single-handed sailing all the more difficult. Fortunately, the sea was like a millpond and he was not faced with the problem of being thrown around the boat. The physical restriction set his mind to work and he began to imagine himself in Biscay with a broken leg, unable to change sails. 'Christ, what would I have done? What will I do in mid-Atlantic if? ... Stop, don't let that crap get started,' he thought, 'it'll cripple you more than any swollen knee.'

Poitín rolled gently from side to side as she slowly motored through the shimmering sea. He limped to the bow of the boat and leaned out over the side to watch her split the water. She moved through the swells like a hand caressing a perfect body. He lowered his arm over the edge and felt his fingers tingle in the swells which occasionally rose on either side of her bow. It was by far his favourite place on the boat, where *Poitín* met the water and made her mark on the sea. He had come to believe she was a living thing with a personality of her own. She was his friend and his partner on the voyage. If he could only remember to quash his fears so as to feel how she reacted to the changing conditions he knew she would always see him through. It was important he gave her every chance to perform.

The summer sun on his back, the sound of *Poitín* cresting along, the daydream world, carried him through the afternoon. Water folded by the bow left creases which stretched across the silky bay – proof that someone had passed. Such moments, he knew, were so very special; part of his love affair with the sea. Like so many times before, he felt wooed by the seductive gentleness but the memory of her recent tantrum in Biscay remained fresh.

How could he not like Bayona, arriving in that tranquil frame of mind? As he entered the marina, the people on a boat which had passed him in the bay asked if he wanted to berth alongside them. Once the lines were secured, the chat began: from where? to where? which ports? and as always, why alone? The skipper came on deck and saved him from the interrogation by introducing himself. 'How's it goin'? I'm Steve ... from Cork.'

Steve was a professional skipper, who spent his time moving the boat around the globe at the whim of his wealthy employer. Dermot and he spent an afternoon going through charts of the Spanish and Portuguese coasts and he advised Dermot on the better places to visit. He also gave a guided tour around Bayona, helping him to find the bits and pieces which were needed for *Poitín*.

The old stone building which housed the Real Club Nautico was an imposing guardian of the port. Powerful wooden beams, supported by macho columns, spanned large rooms which overlooked the harbour. The old building appeared to have worked hard over the years, maybe a naval barracks of some sort, definitely housing for men. There was a masculinity, a raw strength about the place which the polished floors and waiter's beauties could not conceal.

From a carefully chosen vantage point on the terrace, warmed by the evening sun, he absorbed the happenings which unfolded before him. Stunning females, Latin goddesses, drifted through the lounge to the admiring glances of the dark, handsome men. Long ebony hair waved and folded as it brushed against sallow skin while dark mysterious eyes teased and stole loose cotton from covered desire. Boat crews in fluorescent dress strutted about the marina walkways like peacocks in mating competition. All the while, proud parents watched proceedings from the corner of casual conversations.

***

It was his first time in Galicia and the people struck him as a good-looking, passionate race who were polite and proud. He promised he would some day return to the north of Spain with a better knowledge of the language. For now, he had to say goodbye to Bayona and continue south along the Portuguese coast.

At 06:30 on Saturday 16 June, with a favourable weather forecast and a good feeling about himself and the boat, he departed Bayona. It was 180 miles to Peniche, and Steve had warned him to stay well offshore to avoid any fishing nets. With the shipping lane twenty miles out to sea and the fishing nets inshore, he decided to sail ten miles off and stay out of everyone's way.

Poitín romped along to a fresh wind while he enjoyed a silly day, invigorated by a sense of freedom and well-being. The feeling he experienced from being totally alone ignited a juvenile spark which he struggled to remember, thinking it had died in a time past.

Dermot rocked and *Poitín* rolled, to a Hewey Lewis tape played at adolescent volume. He screamed the words at the top of his voice to an audience of scattered ships and passing gull, prancing naked around *Poitín*.

Later that evening, after the sun had set but before the moon had appeared, he sat quietly eating supper. *Poitín* moved steadily through the water. Amused by his earlier antics, he thought what a pity it was the freedom and freshness of youth is so often lost in adult years. Why couldn't people embrace responsibility yet feel free to act the fool without the excuse of alcohol or drugs? As an adult he resented the con-job that society had pulled on him over the years. He had accepted responsibility and worked hard for a living but resented the notion of 'growing up' with all its connotations of growing afraid, or less adventurous, or more aware of what other people think. It represented taking a playful soul and tying it down so that it rarely experienced freedom. What saddened him most was the realisation that these social ties eventually became self-bondage.

Five, maybe seven, miles out to sea the lights of big ships passed. To port the coastal towns glittered and appeared to migrate north as *Poitín* moved further south. With a clear night-sky, and a steady wind, he felt snug and safe in his private world. Pondering the lights on shore, he visualised people living their lives, doing the day to day things. He tried to imagine life aboard the passing ships, with some of their crew on watch while the others slept. And with all these distant people around he felt alone but not really lonely.

The night breeze carried *Poitín* along at three knots and he took the opportunity to cat-nap for fifteen or twenty minutes at a time. Some of the smaller ships passed nearby but not close enough to cause any concern. Often at night he found it difficult to judge their direction and distance but he was well rested from the previous days in port and felt content to sleep for short periods. He felt more comfortable with *Poitín* and himself than ever before. The few bad days in the Bay of Biscay had tested his ability but rewarded his confidence.

The next morning he dozed with the heat of the morning sun on his face and dreamed of home and the life he left behind. He reflected on the opportunities that had come his way over the years and marvelled at how he had always been rewarded for taking risks.

His first big adventure was a hitchhiking trip across Europe. After college he decided to travel to the Mediterranean island of Crete in the hope of finding fun and excitement. James A. Michener's book, *The Drifters,* was mostly to blame. His father thought the trip a lost opportunity and suggested a summer job in an accountant's office to get a head start on his fellow commerce students.

Dermot refused point blank to change his plans and set off for Greece, 2,500 miles away, adamant not to return before the end of the summer. It was his first real-life adventure and he was determined to see it through.

The experiences were certainly varied and sometimes enlightening. In Paris he declined an offer 'to see the bright lights' from a persistent gay man who insisted he had the best view of the city from his apartment window. When in the Alps he hitched a lift from a middle-aged Italian woman who drove like a lunatic and informed him in colourful language why Italians were the best lovers.

Soon after arriving in Greece he made his way to the island of Crete. He sought out the hippies' caves of Matala which Mitchener had mentioned in his book but was disappointed to see they were inhabited by drug addicts who tried to relive someone else's adventure. While he was disappointed by what he saw it was an interesting lesson. He put *The Drifters* to the back of his mind and tried to develop a new appreciation of his own travels.

He returned to Ireland at the end of the summer with only 50 pence left in his pocket. The fear he encountered when setting off alone, the fun along the way, and the sense of achievement when returning home made a lasting impression on him. He had been warned in advance of the dangers that could befall a young person travelling alone in Europe but he found the real-life encounters much easier to cope with than the imagined ones. He did his own thing without screwing up and had been adequately rewarded for overcoming that initial fear.

Some time after the hitchhiking trip he overheard his father proudly telling one of his friends about his son's exploits. He appreciated his father's praise but over the years he had found a harder taskmaster in himself. Regardless of what he achieved, it was never enough and getting his own approval was next to impossible.

Catch a Passing Whisper

Minor undulations on a once-calm sea heralded an overdue midday wind. A sense of urgency dismissed the morning calm, knocking folds of water from ripple-covered swells that hurried along. *Poitín* frolicked through a garden of waves, wavettes, splashes, whitecaps, white petals, all strewn across the sea, like spring blossom in her path.

The strong midday sun suggested a place far from home and a glance at the chart below confirmed Arklow as a distant port. Tickled by what he saw, he rubbed his hands frantically to release the enthusiasm erupting inside his chest. Past conversations were weeded from his mind and replanted with images of his safe return. The sense of fulfilment in his heart helped ripen the resolve which lay in waiting for events yet to come.

Hour upon hour of wonderful sailing carried the day, and *Poitín*, and all on board, to the islands off Peniche. As if sensing the passage end, the wind ceased to blow and left them to find their own way into port. A pang of hunger sought satisfaction from his napping taste buds and then waited; he started the engine and hurried the last few miles to Peniche.

The bustle of fishermen about the quayside preparing boats for a night at sea kept him entertained while he ate supper and waited for the weather forecast. A final puff of breeze swung *Poitín* on her anchor line so that she lay closer to the boats, close enough to hear the hardened voices on deck. Though voices in a foreign tongue, they contained the same manly inclinations, the very same toughness as fishermen from his home port. He tried to identify the steel-plated adjectives, the verbal armour, used to hide the emotional vulnerability which might cost them their pride if allowed to express itself.

Nets, most likely repaired during the day, were already loaded on deck, ready to trawl the Atlantic depths. Layers of chipped paint upon a weary hull which revealed Celtic green under orange and it under faded royal blue, set him to wondering why and when a boat should wear such colours. Rubber tubes puked bilge water into the harbour. Exhaust pipes farted and spluttered from the arse-end of each boat. Plastic bags floated just below the surface like bloated carcasses filled with gas. A blob of congealed fat or grease drifted towards *Poitín*. The shifting breeze had done him no favour and the ugliness of what he saw brought supper to an abrupt end. He started the engine and moved to the south side of the harbour – a little less sheltered from the ocean but kinder to the eye.

A good night's sleep saw him up and about, bright and early. The harbour area which had driven him away now enticed with an empty quay wall as the best place to tie *Poitín* while clearing customs. The water reeked of diesel and dead fish but he only intended staying a few hours – if he could stomach it, so could *Poitín*.

To his surprise the customs office was already open and he managed to dispense with the paperwork by eight o'clock. This left him free to find a bank or Cambio de Change and then phone Jane in Ireland before she left for work. Depending on flight availability, they had decided to spend a month together in the south of Portugal. The sixteen years between them and the inequality of life experiences had not only exploited his sense of age but left him fearful of stifling her youth. They had talked it over but could not unite her desire to experience life and his search for inner calm. The month together was intended to be a special time, free of local society and judging eyes, a time in which to play and enjoy a last tango together.

Everyone Dermot spoke to in La Coruña had reported the Portuguese to be a fine and tolerant people but in this particular town the bank seemed to be where they let off steam. Being served was next to impossible, almost like 'last drinks' on a Saturday night at home. He needed money to make a phone call and buy fresh supplies but unlike 'last drinks' the prospect of elbowing his way through the crowd to be rewarded with escudos rather than a pint of stout did nothing for his enthusiasm. Much like a pub, queuing did not form part of the process. It seemed a nod and a wink to the right member of staff behind the counter was the way to place an order.

People continued to file into the crowded bank and scatter to whichever group mobbed their favourite member of staff. Brushed and nudged towards a particular clerk, he soon found himself in the thick of a smoke-covered mob. A minor scuffle broke out, verbal that is, in the front row but was soon resolved by a general reprimand from the mob who feared total anarchy. Dermot was impressed.

Eventually, he organised the money, thanked those around him for showing preference to a foreigner and headed for a nearby café. An empty waterfront terrace offered welcome relief. He absorbed the character of the old fishing village whose houses were stacked like lobster pots along the shore and further beyond. Tiny quays and fishermen's sheds of rusty-coloured stone were fortunate to have been sidestepped by the new processing factory and the demanding concrete piers on the far side of the harbour. Those fishermen who had failed to make the transition to bigger craft were left to the small open boats which huddled together in the silting shallows of the old harbour.

Watching personalities and characters come and go, he thought how those who work hard, or endure in some way, are often more interesting, more alive, than people who cruise through life. Benny had told him that life was not meant to be easy or hard, it was simply meant to teach us something about ourselves and those around us. He tried to imagine the type of character that lay behind the faces and wondered how many of them had time to think about soul searching. He smiled at the thought of sitting these people down, or anyone for that matter, to recount Benny's story of how people come together.

'Imagine you are a soul in heaven whose time has come to return to earth. You find yourself waiting with hundreds of thousands of others for the right opportunity and you commence the process of finding those who are to participate in your life.

'Your turn comes to move through the waiting souls. At first you are approached by many, with fun in their eyes, who tell you how they would so enjoy sharing a life with someone like you. Another group comes forward but fewer in numbers, with kindness in their eyes and tell you how you will need people to teach and discipline you and that they are prepared to take on the task.

'Finally you come to a small group of souls with love and caring in their eyes. Bathed in their love, you listen while they explain how you will need enemies to balance your life and teach the hardest of all lessons. "If anyone is to do this, it should be us who love and care for you the most".'

Even the memory of the story made his skin prickle and confronted the standards by which he had lived his life to-date. He gathered up his possessions and made his way back to the boat. It was neither the place nor the time to tackle such a new and challenging concept.

***

The sail to Cascais, a small town at the entrance to Lisbon, offered a mixed bag of wind. He motor-sailed for the early part of the trip, hoisted sail for the afternoon and then resorted to motor-sailing once again for the last few miles.

The evening sun added a glorious golden hue to the rambling town located along the sandy shore. Loosely-packed buildings straddled the harbour and neighbouring rocky headland. *Poitín* made her way through an odd collection of boats moored in the bay until a suitable place appeared to anchor for the night.

Dermot had not intended going ashore but the town beckoned, gilded and inviting. He decided to inflate the dinghy and row to the sailing club for a much-needed shower. Just his luck, the clubhouse was closed and presented him with the prospect of another long and sweaty row back to *Poitín*, against the breeze.

More determined than ever, he threw a few litres of water into a bucket for a 'bucket bath', not as refreshing as a shower but salt-covered sunburnt skin craved any amount of fresh water.

Baptised and ready to face the world, he paddled ashore once again to 'check out' Cascais and satisfy the rumblings of an empty stomach. What had at first presented itself as an attractive town when viewed from the sea proved to be a disappointment. Tourist-orientated shops and bars lacked any semblance of character or charm, but what was he only a tourist of sorts?

A family-run restaurant in a narrow backstreet appeared not to have noticed the annual swarm of tourists. Its plastic table cloths and aluminium chairs did nothing to lure these holiday punters who preferred the newly-built 'authentic Portuguese' part of town. And so the locals had a refuge in which to enjoy genuine good cooking at a reasonable price. Translating the menu and ordering took far longer than the time needed to eat his meal but then time abounded and time also waited alone on *Poitín*. The lady of the house, a wife and mother, smiled to someone's son dining alone. The meal completed, he then accompanied a brandy to the point of loitering before thanking her for more than just the good food.

Moving through the streets like driftwood washed ashore, he felt himself carried on an ebb which flowed towards the bay. Shops and stalls as far as the eye could see; wreckage from a neon storm. Tourists jammed the streets; flotsam and jetsam from a bi-weekly tide.

He heard his name being called or did he? Hidden in a plastic jungle of inflatable crocodiles, ducks and elephants, just behind an elaborate array of water guns, stood Benny.

'How's it going, you mad Irish bastard? Good to see you again. Still can't find anyone to sail with you, eh?' His eyes grinned while his mouth struggled to conceal a smile.

'Piss off, I'm happy enough on my own. Anyway the last thing I need is to get stuck with some Aussie git like yourself.'

'I saw *Poitín* anchored in the bay when we arrived. We're just behind her. Figured I'd find you roaming the streets like some lost waif.'

'Did you now? Actually, I was enjoying a most exquisite evening, taking in a few of the more chic hot spots of Cascais and in superb company I might add. If you're very fortunate I might fit time for a cold beer into my hectic social schedule.'

'You're on. I left my crewmate on board with the latest love of his life. Thought I'd be discreet and leave them to it.'

A pint of best bitter served by a cockney barman in 'Ye Old English Ale House' and paid for with escudos made them both smile.

'So how the hell are you? Still enjoying the single-handed stuff?'

'Ah, yeah, it's good to have time to think. I'm not too sure where it's headed but for the moment it's okay. Reading heaps and keeping a diary, started writing too, some poetry ...' Feeling a little awkward at his declaration, he sought to shift attention from himself. 'How about you?'

'Bob, the bloke onboard at the moment, is good to sail with. We give each other plenty of space, like tonight.'

The conversation was easy between them, as if they were life-long friends. It took an hour to recall events as far back along the coast as La Coruña where they had last spoken. Every aspect of boat, sea and land was discussed together with tips for what lay ahead. Benny was headed straight for Gibraltar and then to Turkey. This was probably the last time they would meet.

Dermot tried ordering another drink from the barman but was no match for the drunk at the other end of the counter whose antagonism beamed and lured as if sucking the young cockney down a drain hole.

'Can you see what's happening between those two,' said Benny. 'There is the most incredible flow of tension, that drunk is going to leave the barman emotionally drained.'

'So, tell me Benny, where does that carry-on fit into your concept of spiritual groups.'

'How should I know? It takes a hell of a long time to try and figure out how and why people are connected.'

'That's an interesting cop-out, and I thought you were some sort of psychic!'

'Let me tell you something, Dermot. One thing I would never claim to be is "a psychic". Sounds too much like some-one's "sidekick".'

'Seriously Benny, about that stuff we discussed in La Coruña. I've been thinking about it a lot and there are a few things that don't make sense.'

'OK,' said Benny, 'let's see if I can help. First let me order. Do you want one. Fancy a cigar as well?'

As they puffed Cuban smoke across the counter, Benny explained how a group of souls, bound together by a common need to live through certain emotional lessons, can help each other. 'Not all the group are here in person at the same time, some are still in spirit form and act as guides to help those who are here. One thing these guides cannot do is interfere directly in our lives because then we wouldn't have any free choice. It's a bit like trying to move an object underwater with a long stick. The control of the stick gets a little bit distorted by the refraction through the water.'

'But why bother with all this chopping and changing of people and souls?' asked Dermot. 'Surely whatever put us here in the first place knows all the answers to any silly little problems we might have.'

'It's not the technical answers that matter, Dermot, it's all about positive emotions, how they flow and where they are blocked. We as humans are what happens when good emotional energy such as love and kindness gets blocked by fear.

'The wind's energy for example, is only visible when blocked by a tree or a field of corn. Other energy, like electricity, is only visible when the flow is interfered with or blocked by a light bulb or an electric bar – too much of a blockage and it will burst into flames. A river's energy, not the actual water, its power, its flow, can only be seen when it is blocked by underwater boulders. Too much blockage and it also erupts into violent rapids, which can be seen and heard. We, our spirits that is, become physically visible when the positive emotional energy is blocked by negative thoughts. Too much blockage and we can explode into violence. If we as humans can learn to unblock our emotions, then my friend, we become pure spirit. You not only get to go to heaven, you also get to stay there. All we have to do is learn to deal with our fears.'

'Jesus Benny, you make me feel like I've been asleep all these years. I thought I had started to explore the meaning of life but I haven't even scratched the surface. I'm not saying I agree with everything you have just said, but it's certainly given me plenty to think about.'

'Look,' said Benny, 'I don't want to bog you down with too much of this stuff. Why don't you come by the boat and I'll give you an interesting book. That way you can take your time, eh?'

***

A hundred nautical miles was all that separated Cascais from the port of Lagos on the south coast of Portugal. There he intended enjoying a month with Jane and a welcome break from travelling alone – not that he felt too alone after his marathon session with Benny the night before. They had continued talking after Bob and Susan had gone to bed and long after the moon had disappeared. He had plenty to think about and an interesting book to study.

The day was slow to get started and *Poitín*'s little engine was kept in service until late morning. Once the wind had established its intention to stay a while, he dressed *Poitín* in full main and genoa. A period of trial and error was needed to set the self-steering before he could settle into the usual routine of coffee, reading, navigation, lookout, reading, food and the occasional cat nap.

The sun beamed down mercilessly on *Poitín* and demanded he stay well covered. He remembered a short passage made with friends along the New South Wales coast when living in Sydney. At the time he failed to protect from the midday sun and by early afternoon had experienced the first signs of sun stroke. Incapable of sailing the boat, he went below and left the others to cope. That was when he had the luxury of crew. A nagging fear of what would happen should he become incapacitated in some way had started with the knee injury in La Coruña. 'Stop looking for problems. Relax and enjoy the day,' he shouted across the water as if to chase the snooping thought away.

He settled into his evening routine, not too unlike the morning or afternoon routine except for the BBC World Service which only came through after sunset. Still without the use of the alternator, he had to conserve power, reading by candle-light and only switching on the masthead light when other boats appeared in the area. Early in the night, without any ships to be seen, he took advantage of the situation to sleep a while.

Approaching Cape Saint Vincent at night demanded he stay awake to watch for ships. A busy day could see 200 vessels or more rounding the Cape as they plied between northern

Europe and the Straits of Gibraltar. The same monsters which he had so nervously dodged in the English Channel now prowled the black horizon. He saw no reason to take unnecessary chances by attempting to navigate between the shipping lane and the hidden shore. Neither could he go to bed. He decided to drop all sail and lie outside in the open cockpit to observe the silent dark.

Somewhere in the vague night hours, before tomorrow had crawled from under yesterday's shadow, *Poitín* nudged closer to the distant cape. He checked for ships and sometimes dreamt he was checking for ships. No shapes or sizes, just specks of light slowly drifting across the two-dimensional blackness. Shooting stars streaked the heavens and he gently vacillated between sleep, the darkness and the glitter.

Without the distraction of someone to talk to or a light by which to see, he crept inside his thoughts and those thoughts crept out into the night. Unable to define where body finished and the surrounding world began, he slipped into that no-man's land between reality and imagining. He loved the freedom of actually living a dream. His mind filled the blackened void and found an affinity with the stars which rendered his body alien. Free from physical gravity, his spirit floated through the distant galaxy, the heavens and a glorious nothingness.

But alas, like a puppet taking control, his body pulled on the strings of survival and demanded he return to check on *Poitín*. All too soon, yesterday's night became today's morning and darkness gave way to hints of violet. That hue of morning light upon the stage set the scene for land and sea and ships, to enter for the day. He left his dream world to the night and hoisted sail to catch a passing whisper.

***

It was bright enough when rounding the cape to cut in close and work the breeze as it accelerated round the towering headland. Bucket after bucket of cold sea water helped him fight off the unslept night which pressed upon jaded eyes. The cliffs shone softly in the face of the rising sun and heralded the splendour of another day while cool dawn shadows huddled and waited in the shade of eastern cliffs. He settled back to enjoy the mystery of the shadow-hours.

The coastline gradually changed as high cliffs slowly sank into the sea and small sandy beaches began to appear as if having crawled from the depths to bask among the rocks. *Poitín* moved steadily through the water and carried her sleepy voyager towards Lagos and the prospect of a much-needed siesta. He sat on the lee side with toes trailing in the water. Van's *Bright side of the Road* bounced from the stereo, filled his body with a cantered rhythm and reminded him of all-night parties from his Sydney years. The freshness of the sea excited and thrilled as it shivered through him like the butterflies from a long, long awaited kiss. He felt a yearning.

Poitín entered the port of Lagos as the local people prepared for their siesta. Only the tourists opted to stay outside in the sweltering heat. The afternoon sleep he had promised himself was no longer possible. *Poitín* was far too hot to pass even a few winks below deck. Having dropped anchor in the inner harbour and moored stern-to, he tidied the boat and went ashore to clear customs. He marvelled at the Portuguese requirement of clearing ship's papers at every port, but the officials were polite and the procedure offered only a minor inconvenience.

The paperwork completed, he rambled along the dusty waterfront and found an outdoor café, nicely shaded from the relentless stare of the midday sun. A light wind encouraged warm air to cross the street as he gulped an ice-cold coke and mopped the sweat which pebbled his face. A wave of unslept hours surged through his body in a jaded ache – the sandman's reminder that his escape from the night had not gone undetected.

Through the shimmering haze at the far end of the waterfront he noticed a man and woman pointing across the harbour towards *Poitín*. From behind they almost looked familiar. How many men did he know that were tall, with dark hair, slim build, but slightly overweight? She looked as though she might have stepped from a Laura Ashley catalogue: 'peasant girl in traditional summer outfit'.

A mischievous flutter from the wind or breeze, or an imagined hand, threw her dark waist-length hair and loose-flowing dress from under the shadow of the wide-brimmed hat. Feminine sweeps of the arms controlled the excited fabric while swan-like movements of her head rearranged the dancing hair. He stared, immersed in admiration and felt that familiar excitement, that calm, that deep inner balance which such unique female actions evoke.

The waiter interrupted. 'Excuse please sir', and began rearranging the table setting to make room for the order of fresh seafood salad. 'A coke please sir?' enquiring as to whether or not he should bring another drink. 'No, I'll have a glass of red wine with ice. Thank you.' By then the distant couple had moved further away and were beyond recognition. 'Who the hell do those two remind me of?' he mused as another wave of tiredness swept over him. 'Mmmm ... anyway', as he forked his meal, searching for the lost hunger which had first prompted him to order such a large plate of food.

He woke from a few hours of sleep and lay motionless while his body, like a dancer in the wings, waited for the cue to join the rhythm of his thoughts. He considered moving *Poitín* out into the bay to anchor for the evening and spend a night in the cool of the sea air. 'What to do?' he thought. 'What to do?'

As he readied the boat to get underway the same two people from earlier stepped from a car and began waving and calling to him. 'O'Sullivan, is that you?' he shouted, recognising his friends Pat and Maureen.

'I don't believe it, what are you two doing here?' as he quickly pulled *Poitín* closer to the shore on the stern line.

'So it was you who I saw earlier today, over there by the waterfront. I didn't recognise you in the summer gear. You're

certainly lookin' the business, Maureen.'

Between handshakes and hugs they explained how a house had come available through a late cancellation, 'and when Jane told us you would be in Lagos for a few weeks we booked it'. He was delighted to see them. 'Jesus, this is brilliant, and you know Jane is coming Saturday, it's tomorrow? I've lost track of days.'

'Yeah, she told us. It's the day-after-tomorrow by the way. Come on. Get your gear and we'll go.'

It took little effort persuading him to lock up the boat and avail of the spare room in the house – a much-welcomed opportunity to enjoy a good night's sleep in a bed that didn't move.

Like a ship's wake, the dust swirled and twisted as the car left the main road on the final climb to the hillside cottage. The distant sea spanned out below and merged with the sky somewhere in the hot evening haze. '"Compact but very pretty", was how the agent described the place to us,' said Maureen. "Mature garden and lawns surround a quite adequate pool". I now know why they avoided using the term "swimming pool".'

Sprinklers veiled the lawn with a thirst-quenching mist that made him want to walk on the cool rich grass. He paddled barefoot across the moist softness which tickled with every step. 'This is beautiful,' he said. 'It's like another world after weeks of harbours and marinas.'

They dined upon barbecued food, local wine, and lively chat, all dressed in a rich helping of fun and friendship. Pat was almost like an older brother to him – they had been friends since childhood. Such was their good fortune that when Pat first introduced him to Maureen, many years before, he found another friend. She was stimulating company and never ceased to fascinate him with her sharp intellect and grasp of world affairs. To relax in the company of people with whom he had long since traversed the rocky path of compatibility was one of life's great rewards. They knew what they enjoyed in each other and cared enough about the friendship to step lightly over any stony issues.

Jane arrived in Lagos on Saturday morning. Seeing her again evoked a complex mix of emotions. First he felt caring and happiness but then restraint for fear of hurting her. If only the relationship could have been as simple as her beauty or smooth her golden hair, he thought. Her feelings had bounced off his emotional armour and continued in the opposite direction. She had decided in his absence that their time together was drawing to a sweet but final close. An opportunity for him to be truthful, to open up to another and reciprocate with love, was lost to a need to first find himself. At least he had been honest with her. For now there was the love, the fun and the making of a special memory.

He decided their first day together should be a special treat, starting with a champagne breakfast while anchored in the privacy of their own secluded cove. She told him news of home and passed on regards from friends.

The week passed unnoticed when no one was looking and all too soon Jane and he were saying goodbye to Pat and Maureen. While the girls hugged and made arrangements to meet next month, Pat voiced his fear for his friend. 'Don't take any unnecessary chances out there on your own. It's a big bitch of an ocean. If you don't feel up to it on the day, just leave it.'

'Thanks,' he said as they shook hands. 'I'll be all right. If I can make it this far there's no reason why I can't see it through.'

'Well, the best of luck, we'll be thinking of you.'

***

Jane had three weeks vacation remaining after the departure of Pat and Maureen. In that time they planned to make a return trip to Gibraltar and enjoy some sightseeing along the way. He needed to spend time in 'Gib' stocking up with English language charts, navigational tables and other additional information which might be of help for the transatlantic. Jane needed to be back in Lagos by the end of the month to catch her flight, so they agreed the sightseeing would have to wait for the return journey.

They departed Lagos on the first Tuesday in July, in perfect sailing conditions. Having passed the previous week as a party-boat with Pat and Maureen, *Poitín* found herself clocking up the miles in a sprightly sail along the coast. Jane was surprised at the change of tempo, from leisurely afternoon sails to open-water cruising. Dermot tried not to alarm her when demonstrating the use of the flares, where the life jackets were stored and how to launch the dinghy in case of an emergency. Most of all it was the time spent practising the 'man overboard' routine before they set off which she found most unnerving. He promised to wear his safety-harness and sail with the same caution as if he were alone.

A glorious offshore wind had *Poitín* in Villamora by early evening on the first day out of Lagos. For *Poitín* and her crew of two it was simply a place to shower and have a good night's sleep in the safety of a sheltered harbour. The Spanish city of Cadiz was the next port they planned to visit and would probably take 24 hours of sailing to reach. Jane had never made an overnight passage before and he knew the night watch was better left to him.

What was to be a short stop in Cadiz turned out to be a week of frustration. They arrived late at night after a slow 36-hour passage. Feeling tired and in need of a full night's sleep they decided to rest over an extra day.

The weather changed overnight and the following morning they woke to find a wind, known locally as the 'L'avanta', had well and truly established. Day after day it blew from where they were headed at over 30 knots. Each day when enquiring at the marina office for a weather forecast he was told the 'L'avanta' would blow for the next ten to fourteen days, 'tranquilo hombre, tranquilo, eh'.

Cadiz appeared to be as good a place as any to pass a day

or two. Ancient narrow streets and plazas shaded by enormous sagging palms offered refuge from the sweltering heat. The afternoon sea breeze travelled the short distance from north Morocco and carried with it the feeling that someone had opened an oven door.

After three days they were anxious to depart and chanced heading out to punch into the wind. The next port of Barbet de Franco lay only 40 miles south but with a strong headwind, he estimated a passage of at least eighteen hours. They departed at 06:00 in what appeared to be a pleasant twenty-knot wind. As the day progressed they found themselves pounding into increasingly lumpy seas and far stronger winds than expected. He reluctantly accepted they were not making any progress and that returning to Cadiz was the only real option available.

Two days later they tried once again but were driven back far quicker than before. *Poitín* was too small to make any head-way in a 30-knot headwind. He finally decided to take the local advice and wait.

After a frustrating week, the weather suddenly changed. They hastily prepared *Poitín* to sail and departed Cadiz on a beautiful beam-reach in fifteen knots of wind.

Seeing *Poitín* sail towards the Rock of Gibraltar baffled his powers of comprehension. Here was a foreign port, with a rep-utation of its own and *Poitín* dared approach. His grip upon the tiller reminded him of infant years, as though grasping the security of parental care. He experienced a sense of safety and wisdom in the boat which made him wonder who was really in charge. He felt strong for having made it this far and sufficient-ly confident to declare he intended sailing the Atlantic alone.

Gibraltar lived up to its reputation as the ideal place to make repairs and stock up on essentials. They spent a week there working on *Poitín* and hunting around the shops for the best deals in nautical publications and equipment. He had not intended buying a satellite Navigator, but when the owner of a big motorboat offered one for only £100, he could not refuse. It worked perfectly but knowing how unreliable electrical equipment could be on small boats, he decided it would serve as a back-up to his reliable sextant.

By early August, all the preparations were completed and they began making their way back to Lagos. They took their time, stopping along the way in the shelter of a headland or calling into a marina to shower and stock up on provisions. The evenings were often spent on board simply playing cards and enjoying each other's company. They shared a gentle and passionate time together in the privacy of anonymity and the isolation which boat life offered.

They both knew they could have easily organised to continue sailing together, yet that would have involved abandoning the solo voyage. He was aware of the unique opportunity he had created by allocating a year of his life to the voyage. He had to remind himself of the many sleepless nights spent toying with the decision to break with society and the security of a good business to pursue a dream. He desperately wanted to finish what he had started but the prospect of being alone at sea again did not sit easy with him.

They were both too confused and sad to speak when the time came to part. People shuffled about the airport and offered some distraction while they sat through the early calls for her flight. They hugged and whispered goodbye as the final call forced them to part.

The train journey back to Lagos from the airport seemed to take forever.

The next day he loaded *Poitín* with supplies, did a few odd jobs, and checked the charts for the last time. He was looking forward to the next passage to the Archipelago of Madeira. With a favourable wind the 465 miles might take five or six days. He moved *Poitín* to the fuel pumps in the outer harbour and went ashore in the hope of obtaining a proper weather forecast. The overweight official behind the desk in the harbour office sweated and panted, despite the electric fans which blew from either

side. Impatient with the physical discomfort, the official quickly dismissed Dermot with a general weather forecast of 'no
problemo'. Unhappy with the vagueness of the reply, Dermot
called in on the port police on the way back to *Poitín*. The faded
chart on the wall helped him identify where it was he was headed, 'mi solo, el tiempo, importante'. He thought he had clearly
explained that he was alone and therefore needed an accurate
forecast but the reply was the same as before: 'No problemo.'

Unhappy with the vagueness of the replies he went to the
pub to catch the six o'clock TV weather forecast. Ideally he
needed to see the synoptic chart to know for certain what could
be expected over the next few days. The Portuguese barman
spoke virtually no English and by the time Dermot explained
what it was he wanted and the TV was tuned to the proper
channel, it was all but over. They listened to the brief summary
which the barman simply translated as 'no problemo'.

So with three 'no problemo's he made his way back to *Poitín*
for an early night, reasonably happy in the knowledge that
tomorrow was as good a day as any to head for Madeira.

Days Without Names

The village lay sleeping as the first rays of light prowled the waterfront and pressed against white-washed walls. Shutters, like closed eyelids sensing the waiting day, guarded the last of the night's slumber. Soft morning sun on terracotta roof tiles reminded him of auburn hair; short back and sides on school bed linen. Without wind to fill the sails, reluctantly, he woke the new day to the thumping sound of *Poitín*'s engine.

Poitín seemed to drag herself away from Lagos and he sensed an unwillingness to see the summer holiday end. An hour and more into the day, and Lagos not far enough behind, he suspected the propeller might be in need of cleaning. With three miles of empty sea between *Poitín* and the coast, he took down the flapping sails and jumped over the side with a mask and snorkel.

Around and around *Poitín* he swam. How strange to be at sea but separated from her. All she required was a quirk of nature, a sudden and inexplicable gust of wind to part them. Tingling with excitement at the uncertainty of the moment, he felt an urge to swim further away as if to test her loyalty. And then the fear; the need to rush back to her and cling to her, and climb on board her, and stifle the beauty of her freedom.

Poitín waited as did he, and trust triumphed over fear.

Feeling the warmth of the morning sun on his back, he took

some time to admire her underwater profile. 'A pretty little boat', and she always managed to extract a twinge of admiration whenever he entered the water. Unlike some boats, she looked as though she was made to work with the sea rather than sit precariously on top of the water.

Dragging himself from the heavens in which he floated, the beauty of a boat with fine lines and curves which smiled, he focused on the propeller and the chore which awaited. The longer he stayed in the water the closer they would be by nightfall to the commercial shipping which passed between Gibraltar and Cape Saint Vincent. With Madeira lying 460 nautical miles away, it was time to get moving. The task completed, he climbed back on board. Two hours on and ten miles from the coast, the breeze filled-in sufficiently to allow him to dispense with the engine and set the sails. The wind continued to strengthen as they moved further out to sea, and by early afternoon was blowing 30 knots from the northwest across *Poitín's* decks. In a two-metre swell and clear sunny sky she romped along under reduced canvas. He was forced to alter course for a passing ship which he felt sure had not seen his white sails in the stampede of white caps.

With each windswept hour his hopes of any easing of conditions faded. What had first appeared as a brief squall was shaping up to be the start of a gale. He reduced sail to heavy weather jib and triple-reefed main in the hope of making the going somewhat easier. The wind increased to gale force and his stomach began to play up. Over the years he had experienced queasiness but never had he felt like 'dying' which was how most people described seasickness. 'Saving yesterday's chicken stew for the passage might not have been such a good idea,' he thought. 'Better to have seasickness than food poisoning.'

He tried every trick he knew to ease the growing nausea until the fear of what he fought became the problem. Once the struggle had moved from real physical discomfort to imagined possibilities, the battle was lost. Inhaling cool air to calm his stomach while focusing on the horizon to centre his balance offered no relief to a hypothetical future. By late afternoon he experienced his first serious case of seasickness. With a few cushions on the floor he lay helpless as *Poitín* bounced along at six knots. Checking outside for shipping was eventually reduced to a token gesture of 'good seamanship'. Soon even the gut-wrenching vomits became token retching.

To a tired and anxious mind, the darkening of the evening sky threatened worsening weather rather than a simple lack of daylight. At midnight he listened to the BBC weather forecast, which gave only one gale warning, for his particular sea-area. 'Another 24 hours of the same shit,' he thought. 'So much for the three Portuguese "no problemo"s.' His instinct had told him back in Lagos that something was not right with the weather, otherwise he would not have sought a second and then a third opinion. His diary reads:

> Friday, midnight. BBC4 shipping forecast gave a gale warning for West Trafalgar, force 8. Anything longer than two minutes off the floor and I throw up. Seasickness or food poisoning? *Poitín* is sailing well, no shipping to be seen. I want to die.
>
> Saturday, midnight. Sick all day and night. Navigation makes me sick. Feel terrible but no worse than yesterday thank God. I don't know how much longer I can keep control of the situation. *Poitín* screaming along.

By Sunday he was into his third day of seasickness. He lay on the floor, reluctant to move for fear of disturbing his stomach which ached from the endless retching. His eyes bulged against puffed sockets seeking to escape the dehydrated ache which pounded inside his head.

Hour after hour, day after day, he alternated between sleep and listening to the radio. He preferred to sleep, for his awakening thoughts offered no joy – their wallowing only served to increase the loneliness of the experience. Time eventually became irrelevant; an hour slipped unnoticed into another, a morning into an afternoon or maybe night and the days lost their titles in the confusion. Distance became irrelevant; Lagos lay a few hundred miles back, Madeira a lifetime away, and both lost importance to the struggle from cabin floor to open cockpit.

He craved the deep seductive sleep, the coma-like dream which enticed from the far side of misery but the words of the Frenchman in La Coruña whispered, 'ju most alweys eet'. The words repeated, again and again and again, like a shunting train:

juuuuuuuu ... must alweys eet,
juuuuu ... must alweys eet,
juuu. .. must alweys eet,
ju ... must alweys eet,

until they reached a pitch which drove him from the floor. A few mouthfuls of water at regular intervals found favour with his stomach but food was not yet to be considered. With each cup of water came relief and the prospect of recovery. Although the weather was forecast to ease off by mid-afternoon, he decided it was better to wait until conditions actually improved before inflicting food on his stomach.

Later in the day the seas began to settle and the sun peered through the disgruntled clouds. He lay on the cabin floor staring through the open hatch which see-sawed across the sky and realised he had stopped thinking or maybe had just stopped listening to his thoughts. The same mental numbness which so often fosters recovery from serious illness offered a kind and painless therapy.

The afternoon drifted by in semi-dream; he woke at intervals, sucked a spoon of honey or drank water, then drifted back to sleep. Then woke. Then wondered if what had happened was dream or reality. His diary reads:

Sunday, 16:00. Feeling a little better, stopped vomiting, keeping down a few mouthfuls of water, and can manage some honey every few hours. Must not get dehydrated. Got to keep my energy up, otherwise I'll get exhausted and risk injury.

By late afternoon on Sunday the wind eased back to force four and he hoisted more canvas to keep *Poitín* sailing at a steady five knots. Gradually he began to feel better and was soon out in the cockpit throwing buckets of cold Atlantic water over himself. Bucket after bucket was scooped and offered to his wilted emotions, as if each pail of water contained the very strength which had drained away over the weekend. With each dancing drop he shivered with relief and gave thanks to the gods and *Poitín* for seeing him through. She had proven herself once again and had offered refuge when it most mattered. For nearly three days he was incapable of sailing her and in that time she had covered over 300 miles. He wondered how many ships had passed while he lay on the floor, and how many had seen *Poitín* and altered course. How naive to even consider such a thing. He would learn over the coming year that ships seldom see small boats, especially in a gale.

Dermot commenced the familiar clean-up ritual of first tidying the cabin, then washing and shaving with the luxury of a bucket of fresh water. Feeling clean and a little stronger he prepared a large helping of potatoes, eggs and baked beans. Outside in the cockpit, he ate slowly while enjoying the lively motion of *Poitín*. It was good to be up on deck once again, especially after being cooped up inside for three days. The sky had cleared and the afternoon sun fell warm upon his skin, his body drawing the energy deep within. A fresh wind on the beam drove *Poitín* over a big Atlantic roll at a steady five knots. Once the self-steering was adjusted for the lighter winds, *Poitín* steered a steady course. She performed beautifully, leaving him to rediscover the joy of wind and sun. He dared speculate on making port before nightfall.

As sure as Tuesday's dawn lay in waiting below the horizon, the loom of Porto Santo lighthouse appeared, flashing every four seconds, just as he had calculated. Experience warned him that entering a strange harbour at night depended on correctly identifying the flashing navigation lights in the mass of urban glitter which so often surrounds a port. Sometimes that was near to impossible, as enthusiasm and fatigue could cause tired eyes to see a safe entrance where none existed. Being alone required he take special care and necessitated memorising all critical information. Depth of water, line of entry, submerged dangers, sequence of lights – all had to be taken into consideration. Once close to shore, handling the sails and steering the boat would leave little time for chart work. A well-prepared plan of approach was essential as was an escape route should something go wrong. He needed to allow for possible alterations in wind direction or changes in wind speed due to shelter from the land or acceleration around a ridge. As if that wasn't enough to contend with, he knew there was always the possibility of encountering something, such as a recent extension to a breakwater or unlit buoy not shown on the chart.

One option would have been to take down all sail and drift until morning but there seemed no need to do so. Without any danger of running aground, he could safely attempt to enter the port at night. Around 04:00 he took a bearing off the lighthouse and altered course to make his approach to Porto Santo harbour. The same inner voice which questioned the weather forecasts in Lagos sought confirmation of the bearing. His mind recited instructions: 'Now check the engine oil and check the starter, don't forget to look over the stern for any lines which might foul the propeller.' Methodically, he obeyed the litany of instructions as *Poitín* drew closer to land. To his delight the harbour was surrounded by high, uninhabited cliffs. The sparse public lighting identified the shore and helped confirm his navigation.

About a half mile from the rocky breakwater he dropped the sails and started the motor. *Poitín* nudged closer until the entrance came into sight, safe and welcoming. The harbour looked much bigger than he had expected and appeared to offer ample room for *Poitín* among the dozen or so yachts sleeping quietly at anchor. Once inside the harbour *Poitín*'s engine echoed back and forth across the sheltered water. The stillness of the night was shattered by the sound, just as in Lagos. He half expected heads to surface from open hatches demanding something be done about the noise. But none appeared. Like tip-toeing across a creaky dormitory floor while others slept oblivious to the intrusion, he quickly found a place for the night and dropped anchor.

While waiting to see how *Poitín* would lie for the night he made a welcome cup of tea. The four-day passage had taken its toll physically but he was much encouraged by how he had coped. Throughout the sickness he had not allowed the bolts of fear to take hold or conjure up disaster scenarios. Confident in his single-handed sailing ability, he was at last gaining confidence in his ability to control his mind. Sipping the cool night air across hot tea he watched the steam rise in graceful twisting movements. Thoughts, jaded and embroiled, staggered inside his head but physical tiredness prevented their passage to paper. His diary simply read:

06:00. Dropped anchor in Porto Santo harbour. Bed, bed, bed.

Poitín gently rocked from side to side on the swells from a passing fishing boat. He woke to the familiar rattle of tins, pencils and other rogue items lolling back and forth. He lay waiting for the boat to settle once more. Without the hurry to go anywhere, or do anything, or meet anyone, he took time persuading himself from the comfort of bed. Outside, the harbour, quiet, motionless, with just a sprinkle of buildings along the shore, was calm and inviting.

The black cliffs from the night before had woken brown and rugged with dark diagonal veins left proud by the excavations of time. This place felt safe, a deep navel on a grand big belly of an ocean in which a piece of fluff might hide.

The crystal clear water looked refreshing, cleansing almost, yet it was the same ocean which had heaved and bucked his little boat for four days. The living thing on which he sailed could smile or frown, could heave with laughter, could throw itself angrily upon the shore, or roar in madness at gales which disturbed its peace. And now the element rested and invited him to bathe in its calm.

First came the image of himself below the surface. Then the thought to swim and ultimately the action. He made his way to the side of the boat and stood quietly for a moment. Viewing the sandy bottom through the reflected sky as a cosmonaut might view the earth, he raised his arms. Perched above a micro-planet, his centre of gravity slowly shifted from heel to toe. Carried by the momentum, he tilted forward. Suspended above the water, his weight lifted from the deck. Hovering in space, held for a blink of eternity, he revelled in timeless free fall towards clouds whisked upon a shimmering sky.

Re-entry – crash through the surface into a liquid atmosphere. Exhilarating cool water gripped his skin. Trunks shot up around his ankles like a parachute to slow his descent. Circling *Poitín*, again and again, he dived through shattered clouds strewn across the surface. Without a care in the world, he swam and frolicked in the freedom personified by the tingle between his legs.

The sound of the kettle whistling brought him back to Porto Santo harbour. He climbed back on board to enjoy a leisurely cup of tea before rowing ashore.

Fortunately the Archipelago of Madeira came under Portuguese law which saved him from the endless paperwork required when entering Portugal. While stamping his transit papers the young Port Captain advised that there had been bad weather over the past few days and asked how the sailing was from Lagos. Dermot looked at him suspiciously, thought for a moment and said, 'No problemo'.

***

Porto Santo proved to be the ideal place to recover his strength after the testing passage from Lagos. He passed a restful period on the island. The only village on the island was located a mile from the harbour along a narrow coastal road. Sometimes he would walk along the beach and engage the sea with thoughts. The physical weakness from days of sickness was quick to heal but the emotional bruising left by the blows of fear were slow to mend.

Four days passed and his strength returned. The island began to feel too quiet and he fancied the buzz of a small city. Such feelings declared, it was time to move on, time to find the main island of Madeira and explore the city of Funchal.

With only a 40-mile passage to the next island there was no need for an early start. A leisurely swim and late breakfast preceded his departure from Porto Santo. At first the going was slow while *Poitín* motored with flapping sails but once clear of Porto Santo, she picked up a fresh breeze and took off at a cracking six knots. Heeling to port on a broad reach, she sliced her way gloriously through the water. A few miles out from shore he set the autopilot.

As the morning drifted past, he felt increasingly happy. The sun beamed down and *Poitín* see-sawed her way over the lazy Atlantic swell that rolled between the islands. The seagulls sensed the splendour of the day and came to show off their skills. Disappearing behind swells, which sparkled in the sun, they reappeared with wing tips glancing off the crests. Hovering overhead in perfect flight, they appeared to pay homage to the graceful movement of *Poitín*'s sails through the wind.

'A perfect sail, a perfect day, a reward for the hammering of last week,' he thought. 'Blue sky, majestic rolling sea, fresh cool

115

wind and a sense of one with the boat. This is special.'

Surrounded by such absolute beauty, he realised he could not find fault with what he saw. He felt as though the magnificence of the world was concentrated in that one moment. For a unique instant he became part of that perfection in which he was immersed. His diary reads:

On a day like this there is no famine, no war, no political upheaval, no religious hatred, no future to worry about, no past to taint the present. Just beauty, perfection and freedom. The sea which has been so hard and violent in the past is now caressing me and willing me on. I feel, as we sail, that my spirit has been freed, for a brief moment, to take flight. This voyage is making me more aware of this spirit. It is a far more important aspect of me than I had realised. With this realisation comes confusion, for I sense it is far more complex than I had ever imagined. I wonder if I will ever understand it.

The superb sailing continued for most of the day but that sense of absolute perfection, while just a momentary flash, would remain forever strong and vivid in his heart.

Poitín clocked up the miles until she rounded the north-eastern end of the island and lost the wind in the shelter of the land. He dropped all sail and motored the last few miles towards Funchal. The city straddled the shore and crawled the sides of steep slopes which stood huddled together on an island already crowded with mountains. Antagonistic peaks reached towards the thundery skies as if seeking to disembowel rain-filled clouds which hovered with soft underbellies overhead. Smaller, less aggressive peaks cowered with heads retracted between raised shoulders, fearful of another downpour.

Row upon row of reclaimed terraced land rippled from the wilderness of wooded mountains as precipitation marks upon the land. Rocky headlands jutted into the sea and offered a foothold for slopes to grip the land like toes about to slip into the ocean. The mountains, the city, the clouds all towered above the harbour which appeared wedged into a rocky coastal crevice. Lights from open windows, from outside lamps, from narrow streets and cars which corkscrewed towards the clouds, adorned the early dusk. Madeira was different to anything he had seen so far.

Poitín motored slowly, seeking a berth in an already busy port. All manner of craft were 'rafted up' from the quay, seven and eight abreast. He circled the harbour again, slower than before. A silhouetted figure of a man blocked the glare of a naked light which stood upon a cockpit table. The wave of an arm confirmed the voiced offer to tie *Poitín* alongside.

They chatted briefly as the man helped him adjust fenders and secure *Poitín* for the night. An hour of stowing-folding-cleaning passed before he could relax in the cool of the night with cupped tea and sandwiched meat. The naked light on his neighbour's boat was replaced with the softness of a candle flame. A young woman held a sleeping babe in her arms and whispered across the cradled calm, 'Hi ... I'm Ann'. The man appeared again from below decks with a bottle of wine and quietly beckoned Dermot to join them.

Madeira was not a place he had originally intended visiting but it had sent out word through people he had met along the way which lured him to its shores. Funchal was a lovely little city with some of the friendliest people he had met to-date. He settled into enjoying all the character and charm which that ancient place had to offer.

During a routine mechanical check of the engine he discovered the lubrication oil was a watery grey colour. 'How could water get into the oil?' he thought as he prepared to drain the sump. He changed the oil and ran the engine again but to his horror this oil also turned grey. He slumped in the cockpit realising the cylinder head gasket was probably damaged.

And so began a long and frustrating episode. Parts had to be ordered from Germany and a suitable mechanic found to make the repairs. During the four weeks it took to sort out the engine, he befriended a retired airline pilot called Marlo. *Poitín* was moored by the fuel quay where the engine could be easily removed for transporting to an engineer's workshop. He waited in a nearby café with a clear view of the boat. He noticed an interesting individual view *Poitín*: an old grey-haired man but his slim body stood erect and moved lightly on his feet. Dermot left his writing pad and coffee to find out why *Poitín* offered such interest.

Thick grey hair which covered head and cheeks could not hide the lively eyes and friendly smile which preceded the man's 'Hello, I'm Marlo'. Dermot introduced himself as the proud owner of 'the pretty boat'. And if it was *Poitín*'s attractive shape which helped make the introductions then it was the diesel engine which hogged the conversation. They explored all possible mechanical faults, backtracked to the previous engine check and sifted the pages of the manufacturer's manual for any important information regarding the problem. Marlo understood engines and offered to accompany Dermot to the mechanic's workshop. 'I have nothing else planned for this morning,' he said in a way that put Dermot at ease and dispensed with the need for 'are you sure it's not too much bother?' That simple offer of help from a total stranger was the start of what proved to be a short but rewarding friendship.

Marlo had sailed a boat very similar in size to *Poitín* from England, to Cyprus and then to Madeira. He was, it transpired, older than the 65 years which Dermot had first guessed. It was the bounce in his step and the glint in his eye which deceived. The young girls working at the marina café thought 'Señor Marlo' very gallant.

Marlo and he spent many evenings rambling through the narrow streets of Funchal, exploring the numerous hideaway cellars. They sampled the sweet Madeira sherry. Marlo delighted him with stories of his early flying days which sounded like absolute madness but then he could imagine Marlo as a younger man living on the edge. He admired Marlo not only because he appeared younger than his years but because he looked upon those very years as being young and alive. He had travelled through life collecting years as nuggets to remember rather than sad, forgotten memories in the depths of his heart. His youthful outlook at such a mature stage in life made Dermot ponder how some people live life to the full when others never really get started.

Marlo had a French friend called Valeri who was about his own age and similar in temperament. She was a retired doctor whose first love was mountain climbing but the physical rigours of the slopes had persuaded her to turn to sailing as an alternative. Both were a sight, with white hair, brown wrinkled faces and character which glowed with charm. The banter between them was hectic as they laughed and joked while recounting hilarious situations. Their schoolyard mischievousness belied the fact that they had reared families and enjoyed successful careers. Although they had accepted responsibility in their lives, they had not allowed it to mould their character or quell their zest for life.

Yet behind all the banter lay a knowledge and understanding of life which Dermot craved. They questioned established issues. They were not afraid to modify their opinions to accommodate the changing world. Their courage seemed tempered by one sacred belief – that constant transformation is the only certainty in life.

An issue as simple as the world's dwindling population of whales was complicated beyond the accepted options of 'save them or kill them'.

'Surely there is only one decent course of action open to the world,' argued Dermot.

'That may seem to be the case,' said Marlo with a calmness which cushioned his words, 'but what if whales, like dinosaurs, have reached their evolutionary end? I can't help

119

but feel that the passing of the dinosaur made way for other more advanced species to evolve. If the dinosaur lived today, man would probably grapple to keep it alive, thereby hindering its natural path and the introduction of waiting evolution.'

Dermot smiled knowingly. 'I don't think you really believe that. You don't strike me as the sort to condone the slaughter of any species.' 'Of course I'm not,' said Marlo running his fingers through his hair. 'All I'm saying is that if we are to take any action we should make sure it is done out of love for the creature not fear of its absence from our lives. Nothing good can come of fear.'

And so Dermot found that a truth by which he had lived, a firm opinion he had so often offered to others, needed reassessment. Valeri added to what Marlo had said by comparing the process of change to scaling a cliff. 'Each belief, like a firm foothold, has to be released so as to move ahead. It's the only way of advancing towards the summit. How many people do you know who are stuck, gripping frantically to beliefs which no longer serve any purpose in their lives except to yield to their fear of change?'

He found himself seeking time alone in which to think. He began questioning every issue, every opinion he had ever held. Anything which dared enter his mind was stripped naked and passed before the sharp scrutiny of uncertainty.

And when old beliefs were replaced by new ideas and opinions prized loose in search of new ground, he felt excitement grow at the prospect of discovering a single truth. He would seek out the wisdom of his aged friends. In yet another of their conversations, he expressed his condemnation of the wanton consumerism which gripped the western world. This was an issue he felt strongly about and was sure would find accord with any reasonable person. But once again he was greeted with another obscure belief. Astounded by even the hint that it was not to be condemned he pleaded, 'How can such global greed, such waste of nature's gifts, possibly be right?'

He sat with anger at the ready while Valeri explained how mankind was on the brink of major evolutionary change. 'The hierarchy of human needs is slowly changing. Our most basic needs, of survival, food and shelter, are all being satisfied to such an extent as to reduce them in importance. We are like hungry children in a cake shop. The western world is leading a global over-indulgence as a means of exorcising itself of its basic fears.'

Dermot could feel the anger subside while he considered this new concept 'but then what, what next'.

Valeri's mouth wrinkled where dimples had once been and offered a hinted-smile of understanding. 'Well, when we out-grow these basic needs we will then seek to satisfy the need for knowledge and understanding. Once we have gorged on the physical needs we will seek to explore the spiritual aspects of our lives. Why are we here? Where have we come from? What really satisfies our souls?

Had it not been for the fascinating company of Marlo and Valeri he might have gone crazy with frustration waiting on the engine parts and the mechanic to fit them. It was mid-October before *Poitín* was ready to sail. He had spent four weeks and far too much money making repairs but the alternative was a planned cruise of the Canary Islands. 'You could cruise for years and not meet people as wise as those two,' he thought as he watched them wave from the distant pier. *Poitín* shuffled along with motor running and sails set to catch whatever wind there was for the taking.

To Court the Unknown

The island lights had dominated the night sky and all the sea around, yet surrendered meekly to the advancing dawn. As he approached the harbour, steel masts crawled across the early morning sky, their ship obscured by the silhouette of Las Palmas pier. He estimated the speed, imagined the shape and sensed the power of the enormous craft which lurked behind the concrete wall. A man-made creature with horns held high, ready to burst upon the Atlantic arena, warned all about to stay well clear.

Poitín slowed as he slackened off the sheets. Feeding the rope through his hands the sails began to flap, the boat trembled and crawled obediently through the water. All the while the towering masts menaced those who waited. A fishing boat nudged past *Poitín*, impatient to land her nocturnal catch. A fat lady sneaked closer and waited in turn, her decks still aglow from the night. Early breakfast passengers peppered the observation decks, eager to see mariners go about their work.

Once clear of the harbour the departing hulk picked up speed and bolted for the open water without so much as a nod to those kept waiting. He sheeted in the sails and turned towards the yacht basin somewhere on the other side of the harbour.

The 300-mile passage from Madeira to Gran Canaria had taken only three days sailing to cover. *Poitín* had sailed brilliantly notwithstanding her little escapade while he slept. He had watched the lights of Madeira, as one by one they slid from sight, lost to the curve of the ocean's belly. By midnight all that remained of the towering island was a sprinkling of tiny lights upon the black horizon. An approaching rain squall drove him inside to a bedtime cup of tea. Without the danger of land or shipping nearby he climbed into his bunk and listened to the passing water. Like the words of a familiar nursery rhyme, each splash, each lap and ripple against the hull lured him deeper into sleep.

Lost in a world of make-believe, he failed to hear the whispers up on deck. The spirit of the wind beckoned from behind a passing cloud. 'Psssst ... haaay girlie ... over here, follow me.' *Poitín* smiled, sensing it was time to play. The steering whispered to the nodding compass, 'Shhh ... paaass the word ... staaand by to alter course'.

The hushed command was relayed up forward. Warm air pressed against the sails. Excited, they obeyed and pursued the wind without a hint of sound.

'Yeee haaa ... this is fun,' was heard from the top of the mast. 'Madeira here we come.'

Poitín revelled in the freedom. Her conspiracy continued through the rose; southwest to west, to nor'west to north, to nor'east. And then conspired through the dial; to midnight, to twelve-thirty and on to one.

Deep inside his dream, instinct or maybe a voice from someone who cared warned that all was not as he had left it. Climbing from the warmth of his bed he took some time to observe the night sky through the open hatch. 'Great, no sign of Madeira,' he thought. 'Clear of land at long last'. The clouds were gone and the only lights to be seen were stars which speckled the heavens. Clipping on the harness, he slowly climbed outside.

'Jesus, what's that?' he shouted, at the sight of lights on the horizon up ahead. Confused, wiping the sleep from his eyes, he searched behind for Madeira. 'Lights up ahead, blackness behind, what's going on?'

The compass soon confirmed his suspicion, that *Poitín* was way off course. 'You tart *Poitín*,' he mumbled, setting her on course once more for Las Palmas. 'Chasing wind shifts.'

He waited for the cruise liner to pass before continuing across Las Palmas harbour. Once clear of the commercial shipping he dropped the sails and prepared *Poitín* to enter the yacht basin. Before proceeding in search of an opening, he tied down the sails and laid out the anchor chain. Aware of how easy it was to make a mistake he motored cautiously through the fleet of yachts at anchor. Without insurance the simplest error could cost him his boat and more. He remembered the futile search for insurance cover before he left Ireland. As none of the companies were interested in single-handed sailing he resigned himself to the fact that *Poitín*'s insurance would have to take the form of extreme care and patience. Whenever manoeuvring in a tight situation he would first advise the nearby boats of his intentions and of the fact that he was alone. That was usually enough to get their full attention and co-operation. No need for such precautions on this occasion – the wind had died to a sigh. A clearing appeared quite close to shore where only the smaller boats could lie.

Dermot tidied *Poitín* above and below decks and then sat back to examine his new surroundings. Cruising boats dominated the flock of resting craft, all pointed towards the open sea, quietly watching, bopping, expectant almost. A lazy swell humped the surface, shouldering hulls as it lolloped mindlessly towards the shore. Unattended halyards slapped hollow masts to the annoyance of others trying to sleep. A thin film of oil slicked the surface, marking multiple waterlines on the surrounding boats and the nearby marina creaked from the jolt of boats tugging onshore lines at every passing swell.

Las Palmas city straddled the waterfront and drifted off to the west without any identifying features. Across the bay from where he had come lay the commercial harbour set against a backdrop of naked volcanic hills. He inflated the rubber dinghy and headed for the shore.

Appearing bored and indifferent, the customs officer processed *Poitín's* documents in a matter of minutes – a novelty compared with the Portuguese. Outside, the midday sun promised another scorching afternoon. A nearby bar offered a welcome resting place while he waited for the shower facilities.

The local watering hole was a joy to his eyes. Here was a creation, a notion, maybe even an afterthought. Anything except a business concept. Years past, an old wooden boat had obviously been left to rot along with its owners at the back of the customs office.

Trawling the terrace in search of empty bottles and glasses was a diminutive figure with jet black hair, or maybe a coil of tarred rope which had landed there by mistake. The face; an old brown paper bag, wrinkled and twisted from years of reflected sun, held firm even in the shade. The head; dipped forward and listing slightly to one side attempted to conceal shifting eyes. Thus Dermot attributed the character of a hustler to the individual.

Behind the counter stood a giant whose flattened nose suggested he might have stepped into the ring in years gone by or on a few occasions been asked outside to settle old scores. Dermot presumed this was the 'muscle' in the operation.

The third member of the boat-owning syndicate stood patiently behind the counter, expressing himself with artistic strokes of a spatula on the oiled rectangle which stood before him. A pencil-slim moustache with greased tips characterised him as a Salvador Dali-like individual.

Dermot noticed other customers eating and decided to chance a sandwich and coffee. The artist in the kitchen appeared uptight when he saw Dermot slip his shoes off under the table. An austere-looking cat sprawled high above the cooker seemed to share his master's disapproval.

The public telephone located beside the shower block

prompted him to call home. He dialled his parent's number a few times but the line only bleeped as if queuing for an international connection. The hustler nodded from the far side of the terrace as he placed the sandwich and coffee on the table.

An interesting gathering of yachties occupied the bar, people who would have intimidated Dermot in the past but now a group he felt a part of. Surely by making it this far he had earned a place amongst them. While pondering his standing with the ocean-sailing fraternity, thousands of miles away his mother fumbled with the front door key, afraid she would miss the ringing phone.

Suddenly, his day-dreaming was interrupted by the sound of someone calling from across the bar: 'Dermoz, Dermoz, anyone here wit ze name Dermoz?'

'Yeah, that's me,' he shouted to the man holding the phone. 'Ah, guut, yur mother is on ze phone.'

The bar went quiet or so it seemed. He felt his face redden as he stood up to make his way through the tables. Faces looked away as if to hide their smirks. 'I must be dreaming,' he thought. 'How could she know I was here?'

The telephone confusion was quickly sorted into a chain of events which clarified the situation. Tricia burst into laughter. 'It might just help to keep your confidence in check, stop you from taking chances out there on the ocean.'

'Yeah, I suppose you're right,' he said seeing the humour of it all. 'Anyway, who cares if the yachting fraternity of Las Palmas thinks "Dermoz's mother" is phoning around the Atlantic ports checking on him!'

***

Tricia, a close friend from Ireland, had moved to Las Palmas many years ago. Some time in August he had written from Lagos and asked if he could use her address to collect mail. He phoned her at the hospital where she worked and arranged to meet.

Tricia had not been back to Ireland for over a year. What a treat it was for them to meet and chat. After supper he watched while she put her little boy to bed. After nearly five months of living in the cramped confines of a small boat, it was wonderful for him to observe a normal household in operation.

She introduced her husband Carlos when he arrived home from work. Dermot felt awkward meeting the man whose partner he had once loved, or was it adored. It was all so far back, long before Andriena, long before the young pup had lost his floppy ways.

Carlos not only had the same taste in women but spoke excellent English and was interested in sailing. With so much in common a little male bonding was called for. Tricia was nudged from importance, or so it appeared, but in fact she was given a place from which to observe these men fluff their feathers.

Much as he enjoyed chatting, the lack of sleep from three days of cat-napping caught up with him. Carlos offered a ride back to the boat while Tricia offered a cheek on which to say goodnight.

Back on board *Poitín*, he took a few minutes to write up his diary before falling into bed:

Living on a small craft and visiting neighbours on their boats, one is inclined to get a biased view of the world. I've just returned from visiting Tricia, Carlos and their little boy. It's only when I saw their home that I realised how unusual my life onboard *Poitín* has become. What a novelty to go into the bathroom and run the water while washing my hands, rather than have to balance on one foot and pump with the other; to flush the toilet bowl without having to hold on with one hand while using the other to manually pump out the bowl; to make coffee in a kitchen without having to get in rhythm with the movement of the cooker; to sit and gaze at a TV rather than squint over a book or listen to the World Service crackle from the radio. How simple this sailing

world has become!
Tricia still looks great.

The list of jobs which required attention on *Poitín* was put to one side while he first took time out to enjoy some sight-seeing with Tricia and Carlos. He had imagined Gran Canaria to be a typical holiday destination, full of north Europeans who came for the sole purpose of securing a tan. The southern coastal resorts confirmed his worst expectations but to his surprise, the north of the island proved to be a most interesting place. In total contrast to the hot, dusty, over-developed southern region, the northern mountains were green and unspoilt.

Seeing all the sights the island had to offer occupied a day or two. Distractions exhausted, his mind returned to *Poitín* and the 3,000-mile transatlantic voyage which loomed ever closer. He had sailed 2,000 miles on his own but the passage which awaited involved nearly a month of solitude. Eager to prepare, he began working on the boat and tried to psyche himself to be ready on the day.

The harbour abounded with sailors of varying experience, all of whom were there for the sole purpose of crossing the Atlantic. Most had never sailed an ocean before while some had done so on many occasions. His hope of meeting other solo sailors from whom useful information might be extracted was soon quashed, for there were none to be found. Of the hundred or more boats in Las Palmas, *Poitín* seem not only to be the smallest but also the only single-handed. He should have felt proud, courageous, brave even, but old insecurities emerged.

Placed among his contemporaries, a voice within compared and questioned. Comparisons, long since forgotten by adults wishing to help a stubborn child, were carried into adulthood. Nasty little questions worked to undermine his confidence. Those thousands of miles he had successfully sailed, all those ports safely entered, those fears and gales and emotional lows he had overcome to reach Las Palmas were bullied into insignificance by demons of his own insecurity. Basic common sense told him he had done well to have made it this far yet it was not enough to win his own approval. His father's praise, which he had so desired as a child, was no longer a driving issue. The child was now the man, who bore an anger for the praise withheld.

Anger, when justified by blame, joins heart and mind in a nasty conspiracy of self-pity. But blame removed, confusion abounds and paves the way for a young man's madness. He had disappointed his hero or so it had seemed. He now stood alone, an adult independent in all things but childhood shame. That shamed child now waited quietly for a single word of praise from the hero in the making.

If ever he needed to believe in himself it was now. He buried the demons deep within and smoothed the surface with his determination to make the crossing alone. The pending ocean passage held something of immense importance for him, of this there was no uncertainty, as if someone awaited his arrival.

What had started as a postcard-writing evening in the bar soon had the makings of a hooley. He found himself among a group of headstrong, bullish sailors from Northern Ireland. The crew of *Eevin* who had recently arrived from Belfast were fired up by the freedom and safety of Las Palmas – plenty of new faces around for Dermot to relax, stop focusing on himself and enjoy the richness of the company.

To the fore of the pack was Trevor, tall with golden beard. His big frame was still dressed in a thin layer of winter fat – a bear with the temperament of a Labrador. There was no doubt that Trevor was not only the skipper but also the daddy of the group. Dermot was drawn to this man, who entertained with colourful stories of *Eevin*'s exploits, yet all the while encouraging others to jump into the torrent of yarns he created.

At first, they appeared like any ordinary group of lads; drinks, chat, shared cigarettes and the usual over-indulgence in their mutual admiration of a beautiful girl. As the days progressed he felt three of them were holding on too tight, restraint beneath the surface jokes. Dermot's uneasiness, he later discovered, was not due to his own insecurities but rather his perception of their protective behaviour. How was he to know he was mixing with a British soldier, an RUC police officer and a high-ranking civil servant? How were they to know that he was not an IRA sympathiser who might disclose their true identity and whereabouts to the other side? Their lives depended on their cover as 'professional builders' and the ability to keep up their guard, sober or drunk.

A phone call to their counterparts in Belfast revealed nothing to connect Dermot to any subversive organisation. Only they could decide if he had arrived by chance.

Trevor seemed drawn to Dermot and the combination of courage, skill and utter madness which allowed people to sail alone. His own shelved dream of such a trip was quietly uncovered one evening, dusted off and shared.

Before they could both proceed down the road of their inevitable long-lasting friendship, they first had to explore the possibility that the other might harbour extreme feelings about Ireland's twisted history and current violence. Patience was needed to explore the other's beliefs without a heated outburst. Restraint was required to quickly drop an issue and play out the evening as if nothing had happened, time being the friend of such wilful understanding.

Dermot was fortunate to come from the south of Ireland where political discussions were more freely undertaken. He had been weaned on a strong still of the Republic's history laced with Irish emotion. His grandfather had fought the British in Dublin during the struggle for independence. His other grandfather had experienced the trauma of childhood eviction from his home to make way for a British family. Yet it was his own father who joined the RAF to fight the greater enemy of Nazi Germany. The O'Neills, like most Irish, enjoyed British people but despaired of their Government's policy in Ireland. A confusing foundation on which to build an understanding of any Ulsterman.

They spoke, they listened, they held back, they moved forward. They looked deep into each other's beliefs and found nothing of importance to deter them. In the telling they hoped to be understood and in the listening to understand. The priority was to remain friends and grow. Trevor signalled the end of the process and the tone of their future friendship: 'I've nothing against Catholics,' he said, hiding a smile under his beard.

One of the crew of *Eevin* played the flute and to Dermot's surprise had numerous Irish folk songs in his collection. They held music sessions in La Cantina and he took a turn on the guitar while others sang along. The atmosphere was electric with sailors from every nationality drawn into the music.

It was near the end of one of these rowdy nights that the Ulstermen conspired against their new-found friend. Trevor suspected Dermot was far too sociable for single-handed sailing and over a few more beers decided a pet should be acquired to keep the 'Fenian bastard' company on the long Atlantic passage. At the time the suggestion made total sense and Dermot agreed a small singing bird might indeed make for a more pleasant crossing.

The following day, reminded of his drunken accord, he was dragged into town to secure singing crew for *Poitín*. Breakfast discussion on board *Eevin* had already concluded that a turkey should be acquired for their boat. This was for more practical reasons than simple company for the crew.

Lina, a Spanish girl from the marina bar, had agreed to help them find 'a couple of pet birds' for the boats. The morning's search of the shops drew to a lunchtime intermission. A few bottles of wine later and those who had doubted the need for a singing bird or a Christmas turkey were soon converted to the logic of it all. The search continued through the streets of the city. She enjoyed the stupidity of the escapade and took them from shop to shop until they eventually found a suitably small parrot – a turkey being promised in three days. Lina's disbelief gave way to laughter when Trevor asked if she could translate to the shopkeeper that they required a Catholic parrot and a Protestant turkey. This she refused with tears of laughter streaming down her face.

When she explained that the parrot was needed for an ocean crossing, the man behind the counter described how parrots usually pee through the bars of the cage when frustrated or frightened. The crew of *Eevin*, who were convinced Dermot was mad to attempt the solo trip, proceeded to convince Lina that he would probably stand on a seat and piss right back. A free-for-all of comments and jokes ensued. Lina, eager not to offend the shopkeeper, frantically translated what was being said until she could no longer control her laughter. The image of a frightened parrot hosing down the inside of *Poitín* in a gale persuaded Dermot that a month alone might not be such a bad idea after all.

***

The days drifted past as he prepared the boat for the next passage. Completing certain jobs on his own proved impossible and one of the lads off *Eevin* always volunteered to help. Gary and he made daily excursions into town to check prices on equipment and see if discounts could be obtained by buying for two boats. Gradually, the work on *Poitín* began to fall into place and butterflies fluttered in his stomach whenever he thought about heading out around the pier alone. Trevor disclosed that he too felt anxious at the prospect of setting off. They spent numerous evenings discussing tactics for handling small boats in heavy weather. Trevor provided him with information regarding the frequencies for radio transmissions, where the Trade Winds were expected this year and the best track to follow. Little did they know then that six months on he would be placing more serious demands of life and death on *Eevin* and her crew.

Eevin was entered in the Atlantic Rally Cruise (ARC) along with most of the other boats in the marina. The day of departure, the day which they longed for with apprehension, arrived on 25 November. The ARC intended operating a radio network where each boat in the rally could report its position to a control boat as the fleet made its way across the Atlantic. Weather reports would be transmitted daily and any problems or requests for assistance could be reported. Safety being a priority for the organisers, a minimum of three crew to each boat was required to qualify for entry. While *Poitín* could not participate there was nothing to stop her departing around the same time so as to take advantage of their weather reports.

The buzz around the marina was intoxicating as final checks were made to boats and crew. Grown men and women, hyped like school kids on an outing, rushed about, wishing all a safe crossing. People who had only seen each other in passing over the previous few weeks were greeted with overly enthusiastic handshakes. For the majority of people this was an adventure of the sort only seen on TV or read from the pages of an envied book. This was the crest of one of life's great waves and the ride would mark a special memory in their lives. Sailing the Atlantic for the first time represented a unique challenge. They had varied expectations and abilities with which to see them through but the one thing which they shared was the fear of confronting the unknown.

The bar was jammed with people but the drinking was confined to a shot of brandy or something similar to steady the nerves. Most people he spoke to chatted anxiously, 'Hi-how-are-you-everything-ready-yeah?-best-of-luck-see-you-on-the-other-side.' Their minds battled with uncertainty, with that basic fear, with that human hunger which craves to know what comes next and terrorises for having to go without. While the rest of the world planned and conspired to control the future, La Cantina felt the power of those prepared to court the unknown.

He went over to *Eevin* to wish them bon voyage. They were no different to those he had left in the bar. Trevor ran a check list through his head and called to the others to confirm that responsibilities had been attended to. Dermot shook hands with each of them, recognising the anxiety in their smiles. For a brief moment their minds left the mental lists and allowed time to wish him well for the coming month.

Much as he enjoyed the special moments of soul searching when alone, the wonderful time which he enjoyed with these lads had helped to lighten the experience of single-handed sailing. Just as he was about to step off *Eevin*, a Christmas gift appeared with strict instructions that under no condition was it to be shaken. He held the box to his chest and apologised for not having anything to give in return. Trevor's beard shifted to accommodate the smile underneath and said, 'Don't worry, we'll have each other on Christmas Day, you'll be alone so we thought you might need something to cheer you up.' A cloud descended upon him and a sense of panic welled up inside at the realisation of what had just been said.

Dermot quickly thanked them for their thoughtfulness, wished them safe sailing and rushed to catch his breath. 'How could I have such doubts having come this far?' he thought. Now that his dream was about to become reality, he was faced with the prospect that he had committed himself to something that was far beyond his ability. 'I'll crack up out there on my own for so long,' he told himself. Some of the sailors he admired, like Sir Francis Chichester, Annie Gash and the young Tania Aebi, came to mind and he shuddered to think what they would make of his present state of mind. 'To hell with them all,' he told himself. 'To hell with you, Dermot, just do it.'

He was relieved to see Tricia and Carlos waiting when he returned to *Poitín*. They presented an ideal opportunity to stop the incessant worrying and he invited them on board for one last cup of coffee. Concentrating on the conversation was difficult – his mind raced through endless possibilities which he hoped he had provisioned for. They watched the harbour empty as one by one the ARC boats departed. He thanked them for all their help during his stay and then heard himself repeat the words as if to delay their departure. They could see his anxiety and knew it was time for him to be alone.

After saying goodbye to Tricia and Carlos he headed back to the boat bar to phone home. The contrast was devastating. Chairs still warm from shifting clients, huddled around bottle-covered tables. Cigarette ends smouldered on the dusty concrete floor. Behind the counter stood the weary crew of La Cantina, observing the silence which marked the end of another season, their summer haul now safely landed.

The public phone stood idle – all that remained was for Dermot to call home and then depart.

His father's familiar 'hellooow' struck an aching deep inside his heart. Emotions swirled – regret for the years of confrontation, his refusal to spell b-r-e-a-d, his fiery temper, his rejection of his hero and most of all the precious time lost between them.

'Hello, is there someone there?'

'Yes ... yeah it's me, Dad.'

And while the young man spoke, the father listened to his little boy with tears of frustrated pain and worry in his eyes.

'Dermot, for God's sake be careful out there. Don't take any unnecessary chances. We all miss you very much ...'

The bleeps sounded down the line. 'Dad I'm going to get cut off, tell Mum I'm sorry I missed her, I'll phone in a month's time when I get to the other side.' A final warning bleep interrupted. 'Happy Christm ...' The empty line hummed in his ear. He listened in the hope of hearing a voice but there was none.

Back on board *Poitín* he began the final preparations for their departure. With hands trembling as they went about their work, his heart ached with the echo of his father's worried voice.

Three hours after the start of the ARC he finally got under way. As he departed the marina, a few remaining boats blew their fog horns and crews shouted encouragement to *Poitín* and her crew.

Escape into Childhood

It is now nearly midnight and the masthead lights of a few boats away in the distance make the dark horizon seem a little friendlier. Already I feel like shit, lonely and alone and it's only the first day. Having had such a wonderful time in port, I hate being on my own again. I feel the holiday blues, that empty ache that comes from parting with special friends and familiar places. I have just spent the past month in the company of some really mad bastards and had some of the funniest times I can remember. Now it is all over.

I think I might have spent too long in port because today I found myself fumbling around *Poitín* in an attempt to hoist the sails. The ARC fleet departed three hours ahead of me but I could still see a few boats on the horizon when I left the harbour, otherwise the bay was empty. My first reaction was to chase after them but that would have been pointless as they are all faster than *Poitín* and will pull further ahead by the day.

I felt increasingly isolated as Las Palmas slipped below the horizon but I could not allow myself to get despondent on the first day out. I played my favourite music in the hope of cheering myself up and settled back to enjoy the beautiful sailing conditions. We made our way towards the south end of the island on a fresh north-west wind. I kept myself occupied by

136

calculating our progress and writing up my diary until I noticed the log was not working. The next few hours were spent upside down in the cockpit locker checking the electrical wires in the hope of making repairs. No matter what I tried, I could not get it to work and gave up when my stomach began to feel queasy. I was not too worried about it as I had the trailing log and the Satellite Navigator to help calculate my position.

As I sit here in the cockpit drinking tea, I try to imagine who is keeping watch on *Eevin* and what is being discussed. Who prepared supper this evening? *Poitín* feels cold and austere compared with what I imagine the bustling *Eevin* to be like. I know it is only a matter of time before the holiday blues leave me but in the meantime I feel alone and restless.

28 NOVEMBER

Over the past couple of days I have gradually settled in and begun to feel good about myself and the voyage. I realise that if I'm not careful the remainder of the trip might well slip by while I wallow in melancholy. I woke around 06:00am feeling refreshed and hoisted sail to catch a light breeze. While *Poitín* sailed along at a steady two knots I picked up the ARC radio broadcast after breakfast which reported most of the boats as being becalmed. They have all pulled a long way ahead of *Poitín* over the past few days and I know it is only a matter of time before whatever weather conditions they experience come my way.

By late afternoon I was totally becalmed and with only 140 miles clocked since leaving Las Palmas three days ago. Frustration got the better of me and I started the engine to clock up a few miles and charge the batteries in the process. Half an hour later I went below and to my horror saw water slopping around on the cabin floor. I grabbed the pump handle, rammed it into place and began pumping frantically. The fact that the bilge emptied in a few minutes told me the problem was not serious and I set about finding the leak. I knew I had not collided with anything so the water had to be coming from a broken seacock or the propeller shaft. It was only when I removed the engine cover that I could see sea water was pouring from the cooling pipe on the engine. One of the 'O' rings, fitted by the mechanic in Madeira, must have worked loose.

Fortunately, the water is not getting into the lubrication oil which means I can continue to run the engine for short periods without it over-heating. There is no way of repairing it without removing part of the engine so I will have to pump the bilge every seven minutes when running the engine to prevent the cabin from flooding. I think twenty minutes in the morning and again in the evening will be enough to keep the batteries charged.

Despite the problems with the engine I am quite happy with my performance. I am in good spirits and feel better by the day. Sometimes I look at the sea and realise that if I fall overboard without the life line I will watch *Poitín* sail away without me. I will be left to struggle to stay afloat and wait to die alone in this enormous ocean. I'm being extra careful and sleep with the harness on, ready to connect the umbilical line should I have to go on deck in a hurry. I woke last night having dreamt I was in the water watching *Poitín* sail off towards the horizon. Today my mind started to play games and I wondered if I were to jump over the side, could I swim after the boat and catch up? It was the same sort of feeling as standing on a high cliff knowing that my life was only one step from death if I so wished. The water around the boat sometimes looks so familiar and inviting that I must not forget I am standing on a 'cliff' until I reach Barbados. I must remember that I am once again alone and there is no one to turn the boat around or throw me a line.

As I sit here writing this diary, I now feel unsafe, even though the sea is calm and devoid of wind. It's hard to believe I am now in the Atlantic as *Poitín* floats motionless without so much as a breath of wind. There is an eerie feeling tonight. The incredible

silence is broken by the hiss of the oil lamp burning. As I sit outside listening, without a star in the sky or a light on the horizon,
the surrounding blackness seems intimidating. I think I might go
below now to the safety of the cabin.

29 NOVEMBER

As if to compensate for the trouble with the engine, the wind has
filled-in today and *Poitín* is clocking up the miles once again.
Feeling the boat come alive, having been becalmed, is one of the
most satisfying aspects of sailing. At first, the glassy surface of the
water is broken as a ripple heralds the approach of a gentle puff
of wind. The sails flap for a moment but then die as the breeze
passes by the boat. The process is repeated again and again. Each
time the ripples grow darker and the sails flap a little longer.
Gradually a wind arrives which fills the sails. The boat heels
slightly to one side and a feeling of energy grips the tiller as she
begins moving through the water. The wind is the life force of a
sailing boat and the stronger it blows, the more alive she
becomes. Funny how the very power that gives life to a boat can
so easily destroy her.

Just when I thought I had reached the Trade Winds, the wind
freshened around mid afternoon and shifted to the southwest
and now is blowing straight from where I am headed.

30 NOVEMBER

Friday, the sixth day out, only 300 miles from Las Palmas. Wind
on the nose again. I have decided to take the southerly tack in the
hope of picking up the Trade Winds. The alternative is to head
northwest which would take me further away from the Trade
Wind route. I had originally estimated on making over 100 miles
per day and provisioned for a 28-day crossing, with a week in
reserve. I had better keep an eye on my stores of food and water.

3 DECEMBER

Today I am becalmed once more and am taking time out from

sewing the torn genoa. Friday's frustrating weather continued until Sunday night when lightning and gusting winds seemed to clear the air. I have never seen forked lightning at sea before and I found it fascinating to watch it bolt from the skies and drive into the distant sea. I was far enough away not to have to worry but I still trailed a length of chain from the backstay as a lightning conductor. While I was busy watching the lightning, a strong gust of wind caught me unawares, ripping the headsail. I let the sheet off and clambered up on the foredeck to pull down the sail before it flogged itself to pieces. The gusting wind and the lightning soon passed and I was left with a steady breeze for the remainder of the night.

I wonder when I am ever going to get favourable sailing conditions. I have been at sea for eight days and I am only 400 miles closer to Barbados than when I left Las Palmas on 25 November. Now that we are becalmed the temperature in the cabin has soared and is destroying the last of my fresh vegetables. Today I went through my stores and threw out vegetables that had rotted overnight.

4 December

I have decided to alter course and head south for the Cape Verde Islands in the hope of stocking up on water and supplies. If the Trade Winds do not set in soon, then I am faced with the prospect of a very long and frustrating crossing. My only hope is that by heading so far south I will have a better chance of picking up the favourable winds.

6 December

Becalmed again today, trying not to let the lack of wind get me down. I have my favourite tape, Van Morrison's *Wave Length*, playing. I play the radio cassette unit sparingly to conserve power and use an oil lamp to read at night. I only switch on the masthead light when going to bed in the hope that passing ships might see it. I woke last night to find a ship not too far away. I wondered if I was at last developing a sixth sense, or if it was just coincidence.

My midday sextant sights seem to be increasingly accurate. I check them against the Sat Nav every couple of days and find that my calculated position is nearly always spot on.

I always wanted to do a long single-handed trip in a sailing boat and it wasn't until I started sailing alone out of Sydney Harbour that the dream became a possibility. It was when I bought *Poitín* that the dream developed into a plan. And now the plan is a reality. I have changed my dream world into reality. Does that make me a creator of my own destiny? So far the sea or God has let me pass. It has kicked me up the arse along the way but it has also taken care of me. Most of all it has given me strength.

7 DECEMBER

I woke this morning to the sound of *Poitín* racing through the water. When I went on deck I was thrilled to see a dark shadow on the horizon – the 3,000 metre peak on the island of Sao Vincente in the Cape Verde Islands was visible from miles away. Lucky thing I photocopied a chart of the islands when in Las Palmas, just in case! The adverse winds have forced me further south than I had intended. So much for my original plan to pass 300 miles to the northwest of here! I read somewhere that the islands are extremely poor and very seldom see visiting yachts but I hope I can at least get fresh vegetables and water.

It is late evening and I have anchored off Porte Grande, the main settlement on the island. From a distance it looks a dreary depressing place that is devoid of any vegetation. The few sheds that adorn the waterfront are mostly derelict and I can see very little movement ashore. No one has come near me regarding customs, and as night draws in, I noticed there is no public lighting and most of the houses are in darkness. I have decided it is better to wait until morning before going ashore and I will take the opportunity to have a relaxed meal outside while *Poitín* lies safely to anchor.

Spending the past two weeks alone has been an interesting experience. The amount of self-motivation and disciplining I have had to do to keep going is incredible. Experienced single-handed sailors would probably laugh at my naiveté, but for me it is all new. I have taken myself from an ordinary life in a small town and jumped into the unknown, the sort of unknown that I had only ever read about and assumed was the reserve of exceptional people. Yet here I am, an ordinary man living an exceptional experience. What makes this experience all the more rewarding is that it has not come easy to me. Adventurers have sailed oceans many times on their own but the majority of people in this world would not dream of attempting it. I am on the edge of the latter group, feeling intimidated by the achievers yet desperate to try it for myself.

I set out on this voyage to look within and see what sort of person I really was. The periods of solitude I have experienced to date have set a process of change in motion. I have explored emotions without distraction and without the opportunity to close the door on them if I do not like what I see. I cannot call on friends or go to a movie if I do not like what I am feeling. There is nowhere to hide and I find it to be a very honest time in my life.

Many times along the way, whether at sea or in port, when I am confronted by adverse situations, I ask myself, 'Why is this happening to me?' If I encounter bad conditions, I ask, 'Why am I getting this weather, why has it been sent to me?' Gradually, I have come to realise that nothing in life is sent to me. I am seeking out my experiences. There are many ways of living my life but there is only one life that can give me the true knowledge I need to really improve my soul. I know instinctively when I take the easy way out and shy away from a worthwhile experience. I must push myself more into the unknown to discover my spirit before I can become that spirit. Had I ignored this trip, had I chosen an easier option, I would have missed something very special in my life.

I read in the book that Benny gave me how the decision to set off soul-searching is like a young bird learning to fly. Sensing she must fly she will not know what is possible until that first leap. The bird must jump into the unknown before it is too late, before she forgets what it is she is meant to do. She cannot climb down the cliff face and begin flying at ground level. She must leap from the nest and hope that what she feels is natural and right will carry her through the air. Like the young bird, I too must overcome my fear of falling in the hope of being able to live a fuller life.

I find myself thinking of my old friends Marlo and Valeri back in Madeira. They are people whose spirits are vibrant and refuse to be held back by age. Their bodies are old but their hearts are young, like children discovering this world for the first time. I can still hear Valeri's words, 'How many people do you know who are stuck, gripping frantically to beliefs which no longer serve any purpose in their lives except to yield to their fear of change?' If I fail to express myself while my heart is still young then I might never learn in this life, maybe to be sent back with a fresh young soul and told to try again.

8 DECEMBER

It was good to spend a night at anchor without having the need to keep a look-out, but I still found I woke every couple of hours out of habit.

I rowed ashore only to discover that the desalination machine, the sole source of water on the island, has broken down. After an hour ashore I secured only twelve litres of bottled water. There are no fresh vegetables, fresh meat or bread available and I now realise that Cape Verde is another Third World African country which survives on a very basic diet. There is no reason for me to spend any further time here. I will prepare to sail.

9 DECEMBER

I could have stayed at anchor for a few days and taken the opportunity to catch up on lost sleep but I am better off at sea clocking up the miles. I'm not too sure if I want to get on with the trip or just get it done and over with. When I first left Arklow I had assumed the voyage down the west coast of Europe would involve dense shipping and variable weather. In some ways I felt it was the price to be paid before making it to the Trade Winds. All the Pilot Books and Sailing Directions had indicated there was a strong probability of pleasant sailing once south of Cape Saint Vincent. I had imagined myself lying on the foredeck enjoying life as *Poitín* cruised along in perfect weather. The passage from Las Palmas has dampened my spirits and the prospect of another three weeks of the same slow, frustrating conditions does little to cheer me up.

Soon after leaving Porte Grande, I caught a fresh north-east wind and hoped I had at last entered the Trade Winds. I tried to keep myself busy by having a saltwater bucket bath and then scrubbing out the cockpit. Around midday I listened to the ARC weather transmissions on the SSB radio. One of the slower boats, *Ceados*, picked up the positions of the other boats in her class by VHF radio and then passed them on to the control boat by SSB radio. Most of the slower boats are now a few hundred miles ahead of *Poitín* but by listening to their reports I can get some idea of what weather lies ahead. The small Sony radio can pick up the SSB transmissions perfectly. It's a pity I can't transmit with it. Still, I take pleasure in noting the positions of the other boats and working out how far each one was from *Poitín*. Being able to put a few dots on the chart makes me feel a little better. The ocean appears even bigger than before and when I look at the chart, Barbados seemed a lifetime away.

10 DECEMBER

The wind has increased to about 35 knots. *Poitín* is rolling in a big Atlantic swell and I find myself feeling queasy once again. I cannot understand what has happened to my sea legs. For years I sailed without suffering from seasickness but since leaving Portugal it has become a problem.

The vegetables I bought in Las Palmas are now into their third week and each day the heat takes its toll. I threw out the last of the green beans and managed to salvage a few carrots for whenever I regain my appetite.

12 DECEMBER
Two days of strong winds have passed and now *Poitín* bounces along under twin headsails in a gentle three-metre swell. I should be thrilled but I cannot shake off the loneliness which occupies my heart since leaving the Cape Verde Islands.

13 DECEMBER
Poitín is performing beautifully. I got my appetite back today which is about time as all the carrots have rotted. The two semi-ripe tomatoes that remain represent the last of my fresh vegetables. When I bought the tomatoes in Las Palmas they were rock hard and even though I had wrapped them in paper and stored them in a cool locker, I never expected them to last so long. I have started growing bean sprouts to supplement all the tinned food and to help balance my diet. Food and eating seems to dominate each day, with mealtime representing the end of one part of the day and the arrival of another.

Each day after breakfast I waste away fifteen to twenty minutes peeling and eating my daily orange. The ritual involves very carefully marking eight segments in the outer skin before peeling them away. I then meticulously scrape the white inner skin, taking great care not to pierce the fruit. It is something I casually started two weeks ago but I now find it makes an important contribution to my day. Around ten o'clock each morning I take my time making a pot of coffee and then take at least an hour to drink. I have a light lunch around two o'clock, which leaves me with three hours to kill until early evening.

The highlight of the day involves treating myself to a can of beer and a serving of peanuts while I sit in the cockpit watching the sun go down in a blaze of glory.

Seeing the sun on the horizon is the only time of day when I get some perspective of size and distance. *Poitín* is making over 100 miles per day, yet day after day I sail towards the horizon without appearing to get any closer. Terms of reference, such as 'those distant hills', 'the end of the street', or simply 'over there' are meaningless in the endless expanse of this empty ocean.

While the sun offers a wondrous spectacle when rising and setting, it is the night sky that intrigues me most. On clear nights I lie in the cockpit watching the stars. They offer the most fascinating sense of infinity. Unlike under Cape St Vincent there is no lighthouse nearby and at times I fear being sucked up into the heavens and lost forever in the vastness of the galaxies. Yet it is the moon which seems to smile down and brighten the lonely nights. I sometimes sit for hours and watch it pass across the night sky and feel I am in the company of a wise old friend.

Since leaving the Canary Islands I have become increasingly aware of the size of the ocean and the minute amount of space that *Poitín* occupies. The horizon seems to grow bigger by the day and the sky reaches ever higher into the heavens. I feel the world is being inflated like a giant balloon and each mile I have yet to travel grows progressively longer. Calculating my daily progress on the chart has now become a major event and each day I check and cross check the remaining miles. I exercise extreme care when plotting my position, as the width of a pencil line represents three miles of ocean. Sometimes I place a very fine dot on the chart with the point of the dividers and wonder how long it will take *Poitín* to cross it. I have always imagined I occupy a reasonable amount of space on this earth but I am now faced with the realisation that I am a tiny, insignificant speck. The feeling that all this surrounding space can crush me at any moment is a contradiction in terms, but it is something that is now always with me. It's beginning to scare me.

14 DECEMBER

The problem with the engine worsened. I have to conserve even further on power which means turning the Sat Nav off for a few days at a time and relying on my sextant work. I also have to reduce the amount of time I use the cassette unit, which I resented doing, as familiar tapes pick me up. But I do have the transistor radio which has its own batteries. Being so close to the Equator there are now twelve hours of darkness each night, and I stay awake for as long as possible so as not to run the masthead light longer than is necessary. I have tried talking to myself in an attempt to break the long hours of silence but it only increases the sense of isolation.

Today I heard a discussion on the BBC World Service about the hostages in Beirut and my heart ached. I thought about their enforced solitude and my self-imposed isolation. In comparison to their nightmare all that I have is heaven. Yet the total lack of human contact occupies my mind and leaves a void deep within my heart. Those poor bastards are alone – more alone, the loneliest.

15 DECEMBER

The wind continues to hold steady at a comfortable twenty knots and the sails need very little attention. *Poitín* has averaged 110 miles per day for the past four days which is as much as I can ever hope for. Waking to the sound of her speeding through the water is an absolute joy. The energy that drives the boat has given me renewed enthusiasm. I eagerly plot our position and dance around the cockpit with delight when I see how much closer we are to our destination. At last I feel I am sailing an ocean and enjoying all it has to offer, rather than being continuously frustrated by temperamental weather.

At night I sometimes lie on the foredeck and feel *Poitín* race ahead as if eager to make up for lost time. One of the greatest joys of night sailing is to watch the phosphorescence glitter in the dark sea water when disturbed. As *Poitín* charges ahead, her bow throws waves of sparkling water out to either side and leaves behind her an underwater trail like a wake from a firecracker.

I feel incredibly high now the boat is performing and find time passes more quickly while I occupy myself with daily chores. There is a need to prolong each task so as to occupy my time but there is also the desire to see a task completed and know I am further through the day.

16 DECEMBER

Unlike daily life ashore there is nothing to distinguish one day from the next. Weekends and weekdays are the same and in an attempt to break up the weeks, I have designated today, Sunday, as a special day. A good excuse to treat a day differently, I feel as if I have just returned from an all-night party, almost as if I have spent the night surrounded by people. That last sentence has just explained it – the sense of loneliness has left me. It's great, I don't feel lonely anymore. I will listen to the ARC yachts report their positions, then have breakfast, after which I will lounge around. Later I might clean *Poitín* and run the engine to charge the batteries. There is sufficient fresh water to sponge myself off after a saltwater wash. Jesus ... I'm actually looking ahead. I have stopped wallowing in past miles, past days and weather.

I allowed myself an extra hour of music while I enjoyed an afternoon cup of tea. Busy, busy, busy. No time to let the solitude take hold. Treating today as special has proved a good idea. I really feel like I'm having a break and tomorrow, Monday, I get stuck into the remainder of the trip. Tomorrow I hope to cross the 40° longitude, 1,750 miles from Las Palmas, 1,300 to go. Getting there. I must relax and enjoy every moment of this experience.

17 DECEMBER

Tuesday morning, 2:30am. I have turned off the masthead light in favour of the cabin light so that my diary can keep me company. Having five straight days sailing has picked up my spirits. Mentally refreshed and eager to push on with the remainder of the trip I feel stronger now, more capable of coping emotionally with the powerful environment in which I have placed myself. I tried to send my joy, my positivity, to the hostages but felt myself being overcome by their hell. It's all too powerful for me.

I picked up the details on the SSB radio of the ARC boats preparing to rescue the crew of a German yacht. She suffered a broken rudder and was in danger of sinking, so the crew decided to abandon her and transfer to another boat that happened to be nearby. It is unnerving hearing the details of a boat sinking. I keep my fingers crossed for *Poitín* as I think of that unfortunate boat resting on the seabed. Thinking of her increases my awareness of the vastness of my surroundings, both above and below.

Just as I thought, the Trade Winds had fully established and the weather changed for the worse last night. My day was eroded as hour after hour the wind increased and I was faced with rain and black overcast skies. I was eager to keep *Poitín* moving, so I put in reefs with every squall and shook them out as soon as they had passed. No sooner had I reduced sail than the wind would drop and *Poitín* would slow to a crawl. I then hoisted more sail, only to be faced with another fresh gust that threatened to rip the lighter sails.

All the effort did pay off and by midday on Monday *Poitín* had covered 115 miles over the previous 24 hours. I felt jaded from the constant sail handling of the previous night but I was determined to take full advantage of any available wind. As I continued to push *Poitín* throughout the day, I grew incredibly aggressive. Thinking about it now, I can see that the years of 'will I, won't I' were manifesting themselves in blind aggression and determination. For years I had wondered if I had the stomach to really push myself. Now I am doing it and feel enraged with the 'demons of doubt' that held me back for so long.

As the wind increased earlier tonight, I clambered to the

bow of the boat for yet another sail change. I screamed at the sea in triumph, 'you bastard, you're not going to beat me ... I'm the winner here ... this boat goes all the way ... to Barbados, with me at the tiller ...!'

I gathered up the sail I had just changed and as I did so, slumped in a jaded heap. I lay there on the heaving foredeck, exhausted.

An hour later I woke, terrified. The sound of rushing water made me think *Poitín* had sprung a leak. I was about to jump to my feet and check the cockpit when I realised I was huddled in a sail at the bow. I lay back for a moment and gathered my thoughts in the darkness.

18 DECEMBER

The wind has died away after all my effort to drive *Poitín* as hard as possible. I can't help but feel the sea is saying, 'Relax, O'Neill, we're going to do this trip at my pace'. I'm not yet convinced that the sea is a 'she'. I have watched its many different states and have failed to see a gender. Waves rise up and crash sexless upon the surface without aggression or submission.

Poitín trickles along in light winds and sunshine as I sit outside in the cockpit reading. I looked up from the pages a few hours ago to see a white speck on the horizon. At first I thought it to be an illusion but eventually, hours later, a French yacht passed a quarter of a mile to the north. It was the most exciting thing that has happened to me in weeks and I wasted no time in calling them on the VHF radio. A woman answered who spoke broken English with a beautiful French accent. Unfortunately, the batteries on *Poitín* were low and my radio transmission was very weak. But I could hear her perfectly and I found myself asking questions in the hope of hearing long, drawn-out replies. I could hardly believe I was listening to someone talking to me. She promised to call again around eight o'clock with a weather forecast. I watched as *San Silvest* gradually pulled further ahead and by mid-afternoon, was gone from sight. I am so excited, I have just spoken to another living soul and I have another call to look forward to later in the day.

The wind continued to die away as the day progressed. I considered treating myself to my last fresh vegetable, a tomato which I have watched ripen over the last three days. It is still quite firm, so I have decided to save it for tomorrow and have something to look forward to.

By nightfall I was totally becalmed. I sat in the cabin listening to the radio, and at eight o'clock on the dot, I heard *San Silvest* calling. I answered but they could not hear me and continued to call for *Poitín*. Eventually I heard her say, 'Yacht *Poitín*, if you can hear me, here is the weather forecast I promised you ...'

At the end of the call, she said: 'I hope you have a safe voyage, *Poitín*. Bon nuit, *San Silvest* out.' I sat there looking at the silent radio, listening to the sweet sound of her voice fade in my head.

19 DECEMBER

I took a sextant sight and calculated yesterday's 24-hour passage to be only 35 miles. Ordinarily, I would be frustrated with such slow progress, but we have crossed the 1,000 mile mark, which means I can count down our arrival in Barbados in hundreds, rather than thousands of miles. Now that we are less than 1,000 miles above the Equator, the heat is intense and I make a special effort to stay well covered during the midday sun.

I have a fresh coconut left in my stores, which is good timing for this stage of the trip. I will cut the shell with a hacksaw rather than smash it open, so that I can make something, like an ashtray or peanut bowl. Hopefully the fresh coconut meat will provide me with some roughage for the remainder of the voyage. Constipation has been causing stomach cramp, which also keeps me awake at night.

20 DECEMBER

The coconut keeps me occupied as *Poitín* sits becalmed in the water. I have been scraping the shell for nearly two days now. I sit here like a tired old fisherman repairing nets, making mindless movements with my pocket-knife. The midday temperature is stifling – even in the shade the sweat rolls off me but I enjoy the familiar smell. It is a human smell that reminds me of the presence of my body. I need this physical reminder because without mirrors, or the presence of other people, I exist within my thoughts. I now see *Poitín* as part of me rather than my body being the exterior of my being. I live inside her without distraction from another living soul. For 24 hours a day, all I see that I can relate to is *Poitín*. If she makes a sound in the night, I hear it. If she changes momentum, I feel it. When I adjust her, she responds. I am the mind within *Poitín*'s body. A few weeks back I lost any sense of time. Size and distance have long since been removed from my environment, and now I am losing grip on my sense of presence. All is being eroded.

21 DECEMBER
An eerie calm often heralds bad weather and sure enough all hell broke loose tonight. The barometer gave no indication of any major change in conditions – it all happened so fast I was caught off guard. By ten o'clock I was once again on the foredeck, struggling to hoist the heavy weather jib. The sea had not built to any size but it was streaked with white spray as the tops of the waves were ripped from the surface by the howling wind. It began to rain and soon after, the lightning started. At first the bolts of light were every few minutes but they gradually intensified to a stage where the night was illuminated more often than it was in darkness. There was no need for a torch as I clambered around the foredeck, lashing down the working jib. The seas were short but violent. I sat for a moment clinging to the safety rails, naked except for my harness, as the warm spray swept across the boat. *Poitín*'s white decks and the sea of spray seemed to jump out of the darkness with every flash of light. Before I had time to view my surroundings properly, the

images vanished into the night and I was left momentarily blind. Before I could adjust to the darkness, the lightning would once again flash a blue-white world across my eyes and print an image on my mind. Strong gusting winds, driving rain, thunder and lightning. The seas are a mass of white spray and as bright as day. Terrifying, fascinating, magnificent ... it is now nature's turn to scream at me. Absolute, uncontrolled madness and I love it. 'Yee haaaaa!'

22 December

Rather than take any chances, I am spending today below decks with the companionway hatch completely closed. The wild weather from last night continues. The wind has eased a little, but there is now a big following sea. *Poitín* has been clocking up incredible speeds, shooting down the face of the cresting swells.

Earlier today I lay snuggled in my bunk enjoying the warmth from last night, with half the hatch in place and the heavy weather jib set. Every so often a wave would break around her stern with a tremendous sound. 'No trouble to *Poitín*,' I thought. 'She can handle a blow like this.' No sooner had the smug thought passed through my head when I heard a wave break and felt the boat jolt. I watched, as in slow motion, the water cascaded into the cabin over the half-open hatch. 'You bastard!' I screamed as it bounced off the chart table and poured on top of me. I scrambled to the open hatch to check outside. The half-full cockpit weighed heavily on her stern and greatly increased the chance of being swamped again, and yet again, each time being pushed deeper under water. It soon drained away before the next wave got the chance to hop aboard. The aft lockers were still intact and the self-steering appeared to slowly bring her back on course. An hour or more might have passed while I stood guard, ready to crawl up on deck to reduce sail. After a while I felt fairly sure it was just a rogue wave and decided not to slow the boat down.

Late afternoon – it's great to be out in the fresh air again and feel the sun on my skin. The weather began improving soon after lunch and I took the opportunity to put the wet mattresses out in the cockpit to dry in the sun. The seas were still quite large, but I wasn't too worried. I sat in the cockpit reading.

I was enjoying my daily beer while *Poitín* surfed on the following seas when a small wave jumped over the stern and wet the mattress which had all but dried. I had to laugh as I felt it was just a playful gesture from the sea to remind me of its presence.

CHRISTMAS EVE

Without fresh vegetables and a balanced diet I am experiencing constipation and stomach cramp. I can't help but feel that the physical discomfort I feel is partly my own fault due to bad planning of the food stores. Without the physical discomfort, I'm sure I would sleep better and not feel so tired and spun out emotionally.

The sky is overcast. It rains every few hours and I feel very alone. I try not to think too much about Christmas and how everyone at home is celebrating it. Next year I shall pay special attention to my family and friends. I miss people, full stop. Once is enough. Never again will I sail an ocean alone.

CHRISTMAS DAY

I woke feeling more rested, with a slight lift in spirit. As per usual, I listened for the ARC boats to report their positions but heard nothing. They are now probably in Saint Lucia. I had a small Christmas cake and a few cards on board which were delivered to me in Las Palmas. I opened the cards, read them at least twice and then decorated *Poitín* with them. I remembered the gift from the lads off *Eevin* which I had stowed safely in the toilet locker. I opened the attached card which read:

To Dermot,
This is probably the last Christmas card you will ever read, you

Fenian bastard ...
Happy Christmas!
Eevin

I removed the plastic lid, folded back the wrapping and stared in disbelief at the contents. Four black cylinders were taped together, joined by coils of electrical wire, a battery and a clock. I froze, waiting for the flash which would see me, the Fenian bastard no less, scattered across the sea. Their betrayal, my disappointment, their deceit, my stupidity, all came to mind in a frozen second. Lucky for me 'escape' did not spring to mind or I might have scurried over the side in panic.

I recognised the Guinness cans under the tape, and a nervous smile gave way to hysterical laughter.

I have just dismantled the bomb and poured a glass which I am now enjoying as I write. This is a treat and makes a nice change. I wonder how the Christmas festivities are proceeding on board *Eevin*. Most of them love draught stout and the fact that they have given me what I know to be the last of their Guinness goes nowhere near compensating for the fact that they succeeded in scaring the shit out of me.

Afternoon – the wind has eased back but there is still a big swell running and the sky is overcast, not to be trusted, I think. Funny experience, being out here alone imagining others enjoy Christmas.

SAINT STEPHEN'S DAY
All hell broke loose today. I thought the spray hood was going to be blown off in the squalls. Can't be bothered to change sails so we ran under bare poles for a few hours while the worst passed. Where are the trade winds? Lightning, rain, strong winds. Plenty of sail changes, pretty tricky on the foredeck. Kept the hatch fully closed. Took a few small waves into the cockpit.

Madness all night. Seasick or is it too much Christmas cake and Guinness? Just after midnight I had to steer by hand. What a sight I must have been, with one hand on the tiller and the other gripping a puke bucket! Constipated for the past ten days, my body aches and I feel very tired. God this isolation, this loneliness is like nothing I have ever experienced before. I wish I were stronger.

27 DECEMBER

I feel stupefied for want of sleep. The wind has eased a little but I can't be bothered to hoist more sail. I am so pissed off with sailing, with *Poitín* and this ocean. It is beyond me how I ever convinced myself I was suited to single-handed sailing. Each wave mocks and jeers the courage I might have once aspired to, any fancy ideals of pursuing a dream or soul-searching seem like absolute crap out here in the hard reality of an angry ocean.

The world in which I once lived continues but I am no longer a part of it. No other living soul knows of my where-abouts. This is not a game where I can call on the radio and ask to be rescued. I am tired of this alien environment and how it distorts my emotions. Distance, time, space, yield the most incredible sense of power which crushes me into insignificance. All the years of carefully building an ego, of nurturing self-esteem and self-worth are now crushed by this cruel environ-ment which regards my greatest endeavour with contempt. I no longer account for anything of value on this planet. I am unsure of God but if he does still exist he no longer cares about me, of this I am certain. There is the most incredible feeling of noth-ingness. I have sailed into a void, like some black hole which sucks me deeper into some horrible abyss. Jesus, someone help me. I can't cope with this, I am an open wound, I think I'm los-ing control.

29 DECEMBER

I woke this morning feeling more rested. I am confused by all that has happened and try to occupy myself with chores about the boat. I seem to have lost a day and so it shall remain. Lost in the moments of depression, I have no desire to return in search of it. I encountered despair and will always recognise it in another's eyes.

Thank God I escaped into childhood recollections. I think the tears saved me from an emotional breakdown. I have always felt kindness towards children, recognising their need for care and love, yet I have forever been hard on myself. Seeing myself as a little boy with so much love and affection has opened my eyes. The tough guy that set out to tackle the Atlantic has been replaced by a different strength which knows a gentler side.

The wind has eased but the seas remain big and the sky overcast and grey. I have hoisted more sail and drive *Poitín* on with renewed enthusiasm. Overall I am happier in myself but deep down I feel emotionally bruised and battered. The elements that crushed my ego and ground me into physical insignificance now appear friendly and inviting. The same power which systematically eroded my sense of being now envelops me in the most powerful feeling of kindness and love. I know my soul is of the greatest importance to my Creator. Everywhere I look I feel love. I am the focus of all love, at the centre of the universe, at the threshold of life.

30 DECEMBER

The sky has cleared, the wind has eased and the seas have fallen away. An hour ago, at midnight, I sighted the orange glow in the sky that told me Bridgetown Barbados was just over the horizon.

It all seems worthwhile once again and I feel a huge sense of pride in what I have achieved. I am cruising towards completing one of my life's greatest ambitions. The excitement wells up inside me and I roar at the sea and the stars as I dance around the cockpit.

3:00am – I can see the lights of Bridgetown on the distant horizon. I have opened a beer and share my celebration with *Poitín* by pouring a little on her decks. Just as I felt low a few days previously, I now feel intoxicated with excitement. I have tried sitting down to write my diary but I am soon on my feet, shuffling and fidgeting as I stare at the distant lights that grow brighter by the hour.

08:30am – the sun has risen behind us as we approach Bridgetown. Rather than risk sailing into the busy commercial harbour, I have called the Coast Guard on the radio and explained that I am alone and without the use of an engine. They suggested I anchor in Carlyle Bay and wait for the Customs launch which will call by *Poitín* later.

09:30 – in the gentle off-shore breeze I sailed *Poitín* through the fleet of boats and found a shallow place in which to anchor. I luffed up to wind beside a French boat and dropped the anchor in four metres of water, just as *Poitín* began to drift backwards. The anchor dug into the sandy bottom and I dropped the sails. The Bay is well stocked with yachts at anchor and it seems as though no one has noticed *Poitín's* arrival. Just as I slipped out of Arklow six months ago, I have now sailed into Barbados unnoticed, yet feeling like I have cir-cumnavigated the world.

After 5,000 miles together, *Poitín* and I are now safely in Barbados. The morning sun is now above the land that hides the vast expanse of Atlantic horizon. I look at her and feel my fists clench in a fit of excited rage and scream, 'You beauty, *Poitín*, we did it!' Making it this far has demanded more of me than I ever imagined I had. I feel an incredible sense of discov-ery yet I no longer know who I am. I no longer recognise the old me or know the new. This I hope will change with time. I pushed myself to achieve a personal best and in the process dis-covered more about my life. There are men and women who have pushed themselves longer and harder. What it demanded of them I do not know, nor do I care. For years I nursed the belief that life demanded I confront this particular challenge in the hope of discovering more about myself. I was always led to believe that achievements had to be of 'the best', 'the biggest', or 'the first' to be of any significance. Disabled people are applauded for giving their best and competing, even though they know they cannot beat the records. Yet I was disabled for as long as I was afraid to believe in myself. I had created my own limitations, my own disability.

When all the records have been set, when the world has been circumnavigated five or six times, non-stop, single-handed with one eye closed, what then? The records are there for exceptional people to set but the competition is there for everyone to challenge. We all have a talent, not necessarily better than anyone else but something we can give our souls to. The greatest competitor for each of us lies within.

The Suitcase

'Am I really here?' he thought, as if awakening from a long vivid dream and viewed his surroundings with tired, disbelieving eyes. *Poitín* had delivered him safely from the wild and now sensed his yearning to be among his own. Releasing her embrace, she felt his body conceive of spirit once again.

Eyeing Barbados, he gorged on all around: beaches, trees, houses, transport, a distant figure on the shore, things not seen since 1,000 emotions ago. The void through which he had sailed now imploded, recreating a world before his eyes. The smell of land, a distant sound, the sights, a sense of other human beings, all converged on the tiny insignificant speck that he once was. He had travelled through time and the birth of man.

The ocean had been sailed, the fear confronted and the dream delivered, yet somewhere in all of this he had encountered the child setting out on life's great journey with unpacked suitcase and light in his eyes. He viewed these passing memories with sadness as year by year the suitcase grew heavier with second-hand emotions.

The nasty little questions which had threatened to sour his departure from Las Palmas were consumed by a burning sense of achievement. Applause resounded inside his heart, tears of fulfilment ejaculated from deep, deep within his soul and words of praise were quietly uttered to the self-made hero. He exalted the child above all shame for the suitcase had at last been opened and the contents uncovered.

A strong but gentle inner peace came over him and left no doubt he had given his best. Never had he experienced such excitement and calm simultaneously, as though a wise and ancient soul watched from afar while the child frolicked in the morning sun. Les was right, he thought, remembering their conversation from before his departure: 'Life is a journey where someone else packs your luggage.' He listened to his mind recite the emotional vocabulary, the litany of phrases whose truth he once feared, phrases that lurked behind the columns of his conviction, hiding in wait for opportunities; those moments of human weakness when strength is confronted by baleful self-doubt, as words spoken by parents to children, or teachers to students, or priest to parishioners, or aunts to nieces, or grandparents to grandchildren to great-grandchildren to the greatest of children in their journey through the ages, words which confront the sweet seductive smell of invincibility with the rancidity of imagined failure.

But he had gone beyond the Pillars of Hercules, challenged the unknown, the self-ridicule, to emerge the vanquisher of fear. Overcome with relief, he plonked upon the cockpit seat as the weeks of tension eased their grip and drained from his jaded limbs. The realisation that he was safely in port aroused thoughts of endless slumber. Tonight he could sleep without concern for bad weather, for keeping watch, for loneliness or sails that demanded to be changed. He could go ashore, stay ashore, not return for the entire night or do whatever took his fancy.

As he looked around the bay, enjoying the colours of the other boats, an inflatable dinghy sped in his direction. The driver waved and soon he recognised Denis, the silhouetted figure from his first night in Madeira. No sooner had the tender rested beside *Poitín* than Dermot grasped his hand and shook it with such enthusiasm that the owner was forced to plead for its safe return. His excitement precluded any coherent conversation as words spewed forth in a continuous bombardment of questions which Denis stood no hope of answering. He caught the sound of his own voice and chuckled and spoke a little louder, and laughed, and heard his sounds above Denis' drowning words.

Denis decided to take control of the situation. 'Just lock up the boat and get in the dinghy,' he demanded.

The catamaran seemed enormous after *Poitín*'s cramped little cabin. Ann moved to greet him while trying not to disturb the sleeping child. 'You're not still holding that baby,' he jibed, hugging her for far longer than new friends might and in his enthusiasm failed to heed her embarrassed movement.

While Denis prepared breakfast they chatted about their respective ocean crossings. Where Dermot had followed the text-book route in hope of good weather, they had taken the unusual decision to sail directly from Madeira and had been rewarded with perfect trade-wind sailing.

Having spent weeks in the sole company of his mind, Dermot was once again among people and of this he demanded reassurance. He moved about the boat from one to the other, chatting, stealing physical contact, and seeking understanding with a smile. Ann suggested he might like to use the shower before breakfast, and it slowly dawned on him that the familiar smell which had served as a reminder of his physical body was not so welcome. He needed a wash and a shave, and even some fresh food but most of all he needed people.

The customs launch arrived while Dermot busied himself rearranging *Poitín* in preparation for a long stay in port. Once the paperwork was complete he launched the dinghy for the row ashore, where an old converted boatyard served as a bar, a clubhouse and a mail collection point. Rowing into the warm midday breeze, he watched *Poitín* drift to and fro; her mast bare, her sails stowed, her tiller tied and she all but empty except for a part of him.

'Strange thing to be looking back when approaching a new

place,' he thought, pulling hard on the oars to catch a surge. The dinghy tilted forward and slid on the face of a swell that aspired to wavehood but then stumbled on the shore. He stepped onto the golden sand and reacquainted himself with the feel of the earth under his feet. A wave broke and swirled about his legs as if to pull him seaward or seeking to be remembered and thanked for allowing him to pass.

He pulled the dinghy into the shade of the dilapidated wooden jetty which had once joined boatyard to sea in some useful purpose and looked with trepidation at the lunch time crowd gathered at the outdoor bar. 'And after 30 days and 30 nights they threw him to the masses,' he thought, feeling the need to reacquaint himself with people. 'Let's see what this lot have in store for me.'

Not a familiar face was to be seen as he advanced through the scattered tables towards the bar, his sun-bleached eyes growing accustomed to the shade. Behind the counter stood a divine creature and in his mind she was undressed except for tight jeans, sleeveless T-shirt and a gold neck chain which accentuated the smoothness of her dark skin. She saw the madness in his eyes, panicked and somehow vanished while he paused to search through his wallet.

In her place appeared an enormous figure, a matriarch with a face to rival the bark of a coconut tree. Slowly raising his head to place an order, he jolted at the transformation, tripped backwards, and landed on the floor. Perplexed by the sorcery of the place he watched in disbelief as two hairy male legs moved quickly towards him. A strong male hand helped restore him to his feet and its owner listened with amusement while he pleaded his sobriety to the guardian of the bar.

'Have you just arrived?' asked the helping hand.

Thus he met Simon, who in turn introduced him to 'Mad Terry'. Rising from the table to greet him, Terry squeezed a big welcome into his hand and offered a bearded smile which would forever define him as an older Trevor-like character. He looked into the face of this big man with greying hair, bespectacled eyes and teeth which grinned without knowing, and felt very much at ease.

Terry had sailed single-handed from Dublin and to Dermot's surprise had no intentions of sailing another mile alone if he could possibly avoid it. They agreed that single-handed sailing was more suited to solitary individuals.

They talked with ease, their common experience supplanting the need for shared years to establish a friendship bond. The hours slipped by unnoticed as they shared for the first time the privacy of their time alone but neither was surprised to discover how similar their lives had been while at sea. They touched on loneliness, as best men can without the help of female honesty to explore such emotions. He skirted the subject of depression but quickly changed tack when he discovered it had not formed part of Terry's experience, or so he said.

Denis and Ann joined the table and brought with them a few new faces for him to meet. The conversation gained in momentum as stories were traded and with each shared encounter, strangers were made to feel more familiar.

'One morning after breakfast, when I was becalmed in the doldrums,' said Terry, 'I tossed the grapefruit peel over the side only to see the bloody thing still floating there beside the boat at eight o'clock that evening.'

'Hold it a second,' interrupted Dermot, 'what were you doing that far south?'

'Well, to be honest, I was on my way here from Brazil ...'

'Brazil? I thought you said you'd sailed from Dublin? How'd you end up in the South Atlantic?

'It's a long story,' said Terry, half embarrassed, half enthusiastic at the prospect of disclosing the facts. So, having inadvertently reversed into the story, Terry had no choice but to start at the beginning.

It transpired that he was attempting to circumnavigate the globe by way of Cape Horn and was not headed for the Panama Canal as Dermot had assumed. Anyway, when approaching the coast of Brazil, he was overcome with tiredness and slipped into a deep exhausted sleep – this Dermot fully understood. He later woke to the sound of water lapping as his boat, *Peg,* was pushed towards the shore. He struggled throughout the night to save her but by dawn the ebb tide had left her high and dry on a sandy beach. Fortunately, she was not damaged and a Brazilian Naval vessel which had arrived on the scene very kindly waited for the next flood tide to tow her off.

'I couldn't believe my luck,' said Terry. 'One minute there's the prospect of a long walk home, and the next minute I find I'm safely moored in a naval dockyard, courtesy of the Brazilian Navy.

'The only problem was that someone in authority soon took a shine to *Peg* and had her impounded without my knowledge. So while I was busy preparing *Peg* for sea again, someone else was happily watching their new toy being repaired.

'It didn't take too long for me to twig what was planned for *Peg.* So each day when I went shopping I bought extra stores but never enough to attract attention. Then on New Year's Eve, at the height of the celebrations I slipped out of there.'

A cheer went up from around the table in praise of such daring and Terry thumbed his nose in triumph.

By now another table had been pulled over to facilitate the growing numbers and the lunch plates removed to make way for sundowners. Sitting under the flapping palm trees which offered no protection from the late afternoon sun, stories were traded.

The young girl, the divine creature, who worked in the bar, appeared at the table and asked for him by name. 'Dermot O'Neill, on a boat called *Poitín.*' His heart jumped. 'Yeah ... yes that's me,' he declared.

'This mail arrived a few days ago,' she said nervously,

trying to avoid eye contact. A little disappointed yet relieved, he took possession of a few letters and a package about the size of a small football. The conversation resumed around the table while he proceeded to remove the wrapping but they could not help glancing casually in his direction, drawn by the anticipation which accompanies the opening of all gifts.

'Oh Jesus, not again,' he mumbled as he read the enclosed card. The conversation died completely, and the questions began.

'What is it?'

'Who's it from?'

'What's so funny?'

'I'll strangle her,' he thought while holding up the gift for all to see. 'It's a home-made Christmas pudding from my mother.'

'Ahh, isn't that sweet,' said Terry. 'Does your mammy send you many food parcels?'

Dermot sat with the pudding held in mock embrace while the barrage of orders for Mammy O'Neill's Food Delivery Service flew around the table. Soon the whole bar was focused on Mrs O'Neill's hungry little boy.

'Shag off, the lot of you,' he said, 'or I won't share it.'

As the bar continued to fill with people and the level of activity steadily grew he found it increasingly difficult to cope with the rising noise. He had spent the past month in the quiet sanctuary that was *Poitín* and his ears had grown accustomed to the sound of the sea and the inner whisper of his thoughts. His voice, which had also rested for the long ocean crossing, struggled with the sudden and constant use. His eyes, having found comfort in the subtleties of sea and sky, were dazed by the lights and their reflections. Soon he was forced to abandon his new-found friends and seek refuge on *Poitín*.

Dermot had passed the last week of the voyage thinking he would never get ashore, yet he was alone again on board taking solace in the very isolation he had grown to fear. A strange and

confusing compulsion to savour once more the madness from
hence he had come hinted there might no longer be a place for
him in society. Vacating the darkness of the cabin, he moved to
the bow where the warm night air caressed his skin and the
reflected lights helped calm his thoughts. He told himself that
the desire for solitude and the feeling of not being able to cope
with crowds would soon pass and he would be back to his
sociable self in a few days. 'It's probably the effect of the few
beers,' he thought.

Before going to bed he wrote up his diary which he found
amusing to read the following morning:

30 DECEMBER

How strange it is to have experienced what I have during the
past month. Yet another lesson in life I suppose. Funny how
there is never an end-of-year sale with life's experiences. All
life's lessons are at top price. You don't have to buy but when
you do it's always value for money. No 50% end-of-year sale,
no £9.99 offers at life's counter, no sir. Only when we pay the
full price do we get top goods. 'How much is that God ... Sir?'
'That'll cost five units of fun, ten units of emotional upset, a kick
in the knackers and that's a special to you Dermo.'

'I'll take it.'

***

Carlyle Bay offered a unique paradise location on the edge of
Bridgetown but he was confounded as to how such a place had
gone unnoticed by the city developers. Palm trees stood high
above the assorted houses and empty plots that loitered
around the bay, their scrub extending to the sun-bleached sand.
He could not have hoped for a more beautiful environment in
which to relax and reacquaint himself with people after the
crossing. With each passing night he slept a little longer and
without the frequent awakenings that had jolted him to check

that all was well outside.

Each morning he woke to the sounds of heaven passing his ears and lay for a while to converse with the God who had found him alone in the ocean and kissed his soul. In those precious moments when his mind still slept, a calm emanated from within and he felt the purest of all emotions, his own love.

On such a morning, he recalled his escape from mid-ocean depression into childhood years and remembered being cradled in his father's arms, before the b-r-e-a-d bin had come between them. He drifted into sleep once more but in a dream, he was the hero who held the child and offered comfort and love with which to fight ancestral fears.

And this was how the cradled child, the shamed boy, the angry man, put aside all blame and took upon himself the responsibility of parenthood. He had held the child and saw love before life had made a mark. No longer could he look to others or point to past events to excuse his own self-ridicule. He gained in love and understanding of himself and in so doing altered his attitude to people, sensing their vulnerability behind life's armour. This compassion towards others reflected his new appreciation that for many, maturity simply meant encasing their souls in layer upon layer of adult fears.

Of all the people he met in Barbados, Denis and Ann were the calmest and most profound and so it was with them one evening after supper that he chose to share his thoughts. They listened patiently while he revealed the intrinsic detail of his dream and soon the softness in their faces intimated their understanding.

Having discussed Denis' apprehension and fears at the thought of becoming a parent, Dermot asked in a hushed half-whisper, 'How do you intend rearing your little girl ... I mean, how can you avoid introducing her to possible dangers?'

'All we can do,' said Denis, 'is to make her aware of the emotional fears which exist so that at least she can see the enemy within, the hidden demons of the mind. What I refuse to do is instil fear into her and thereby give these demons real power. I would like her to know that something as infuriating as snobbery, for example, is simply fear of social rejection, that greed is the fear of not having enough, that the need to dominate is the fear of being dominated, that ridicule is the fear of being ridiculed, etc, etc. I would like her to confront negativity and evil with understanding first and then action ... understand your enemy and the conflict is almost won, right?'

They talked late into the night and Dermot found himself offering some of Benny's ideas as possible answers to the questions raised. He heard the words pass from his mouth and realised that having pondered their truth for so long, they were not only acceptable but formed part of his beliefs.

Dermot took full advantage of the perfect setting in which he woke each day, diving into the early light which glistened on the bejewelled sea. He set up the cockpit table outside in the warm whispers of the morning breeze and invited a few friends for breakfast. This soon became a regular occurrence, as more and more people dropped by for coffee on their way ashore and the ritual extended later into the morning. Some would swim to *Poitín* from nearby boats while others arrived by dinghy. Terry, who was anchored closer than any of the other breakfast visitors, but was dinghyless as a result of his Brazilian detour, used to whistle to be collected.

He was glad to have first met Terry on his arrival and not Ricardo, a young single-handed sailor from Spain who was later introduced to the company. In contrast to Dermot and Terry, Ricardo never experienced loneliness nor had any desire to take on crew. Even when in port after the long ocean passage he preferred to pass many hours alone on the boat practising music. A superb flautist, good enough to have once played with an orchestra in Barcelona, he named his boat *Frédéric Chopin*. On the quieter evenings at the boatyard he would venture a few hours ashore, where flute or trumpet, guitar or lilting voice, tambourine or tapping hand, found a tune or two in common among those who had gathered to share their talents. He would sit quietly to one side, accompanying whoever had chosen to lead but as the evening drew to a close and when all possibilities were exhausted and the instruments laid aside or taken home to bed, he could sometimes be persuaded to play his own compositions. To watch him was a thing of beauty. His strong Moorish features and sapphirine eyes bewitched those already enthralled by his musical alchemy. With slim lips stretched, he kissed each glancing breath that swept to greet the elegance of his fingers as they danced upon the waiting keys. His lank neglected body did nothing to deter the female admirers whose souls were drawn by the tender puissance demanded by such a score but they failed to see the all-consuming lover held closely to his mouth.

All too soon boats began leaving Carlyle Bay to cruise the chain of islands that stretched from South America to the USA and Dermot knew it was only a matter of days before he would set sail once again. He was saddened by the daily farewells that marked the end of a warm and friendly experience in his travels. People like Denis and Ann he would see along the way but many were headed in opposite directions.

Just as the boatyard began to feel empty, Ricardo introduced him to two American girls who had flown to Barbados from Grenada on the second leg of their Caribbean holiday. They passed their first afternoon together on the beach and shared an easiness so familiar that neither the long lazy silences nor their unannounced comings and goings to the water's edge offended the conversation. Five months had passed since Jane and he parted company in Lagos and the recollection of those tender moments sublimated his need of all things female.

He watched Brigit walk towards the water and observed her feet twisting in the soft dry sand. His breathing quickened as she moved through the shallow water, her thighs awash and her fingertips touching the surface as if to mark a trail so one might follow. He beheld the pleasure of her image as she fell

170

into the embrace of the silky ocean and was lost to the reflected glare of the sun.

It was late afternoon when Ricardo prepared to depart for another evening of music alone on *Frédéric Chopin*. Dermot refused to let the day finish so abruptly and quickly suggested Brigit and Nina join him on *Poitín* where he was sure he could muster up something for supper.

The girls sat outside in the cockpit enjoying the view of the bay while he contemplated the three lockers and two-ringed camping cooker that constituted *Poitín*'s galley. The nature of the original dinner invitation was far superior to the menu. His proposal of fried eggs, mashed potatoes and something or other from a tin received a look of pity and he was duly persuaded from the galley to lay the table outside.

The light from the lantern on the cockpit table flickered upon their bronzed faces while they sipped wine after supper and enjoyed an honest conversation, as though they were old friends who would not meet again for many years. There was no doubt he was attracted to Brigit but he noticed something different in his attitude towards her. He had loved many women over the years, often treating them badly when the relationship demanded true intimacy. The Atlantic had revealed to him how fragile all hearts are and he realised he could no longer hide behind his tough guy's façade.

The boatyard was almost empty when later that evening he rowed them both ashore in time to catch a taxi back to their hotel. Before leaving he suggested they should consider sailing to Grenada on *Poitín* rather than returning by plane. 'We could stop at a few islands along the way,' he said, trying not appear too enthusiastic.

***

The last Saturday in January saw *Poitín* tow *Frédéric Chopin* to the Customs Office in the main shipping harbour prior to leaving Barbados. He felt a pang of anxiety at the prospect of leaving the safety of Carlyle Bay, for only a month past he had begged to be rid of *Poitín* and far removed from any ocean.

He had stayed in Barbados long enough to make new friends and to become familiar with his surroundings. The communal sense of achievement at having crossed the ocean and the excitement at the prospect of exploring the Caribbean Islands ensured all would remember it as a special place. He was fortunate to have shared in a unique frame of mind, a group experience that seldom occurs and is never forgotten.

Brigit and Nina waved to *Frédéric Chopin* and laughed excitedly as *Poitín* moved further from the shore. He couldn't help but feel for Ricardo sailing alone when he might have shared that beautiful day with someone else but he had made it clear he had no need of crew.

Nina had sailed before and was eager to take the tiller once *Poitín* was clear of land. He enjoyed the opportunity to show them both the pleasure of *Poitín* in such glorious conditions. All too often he had seen people introduced to sailing in weather conditions that stood to frighten the novice and satisfy some perverted belief on the part of the expert that sailing had to be tough to be fun.

To celebrate her return to the ocean *Poitín* received a fresh wind to fill her sails, a gentle sea to whet her hull and a rich blue sky to cheer her on her way. For him such days were nature's feminine touch upon the earth and the dancing sails the stuff of fine ballet upon a stage. He tacked *Poitín* from side to side as if in preparation for an opening night's performance. She passed *Frédéric Chopin* in long inviting sweeps so that Ricardo might see his passion for sailing through the beauty of such movements and be persuaded to partake in a little *pas de deux*.

The two boats glanced across the surface towards each other. Passing to port, they spun on pointed keels in tight pirouette, and luffing up to wind their sails trembled. Ricardo then turned *Frédéric Chopin* and followed *Poitín* in a long steady sweep which saw the two boats on their way.

Barbados was all but gone from view as the last of the setting sun oozed molten lava across the horizon and the night that followed from behind drained all colour from the clear day's sky. This changing brought a hint of apprehension among those on board which prevailed until they grew acquainted with the assertive black of night.

Long after the taste of supper had left their buds, a half-bellied moon rose into the sky and, like a mariner's course drawn across a chart, marked a path of light by which to steer. Dermot decided it was time to plan the night and left the girls on watch for a few hours while he slept, on the understanding that they would call should anything appear on the horizon.

He woke before midnight and lay for a moment to hear the soft, whispered voices from outside mingle with the rush of water against the hull. Nina was first to bed while Brigit remained outside in the warm night air and talked to him of her life in a small country town. 'You know they're not going to believe we just took off in a small boat with some guy we only met two days before,' she said, staring into the winking stars, 'but I'll tell you one thing, they would sure laugh if I told them I believed my guardian angel was looking after me and had helped to make all this happen.' It was her guiding spirit whom she claimed had given her the strength to make it through the heartache of a recent divorce and would always be there to help her through life. He enjoyed her honesty and listened with great interest while she described how she had continued to believe in a spiritual guide long after she was old enough to take care of herself.

The girls slept as *Poitín* moved ever closer to the island of Bequia that lay somewhere beyond the distant horizon, now dark and unseen by the passing of the moon. He tried to imagine what lay ahead in the coming months as he sailed *Poitín* through the Caribbean and the thousands of miles to be crossed on his way home to Ireland.

Brigit and Nina eventually appeared feeling tired yet buzzing with excitement at the sight of the horizon ahead and the land that lay sleeping under early morning clouds. Nina set about making breakfast while Brigit folded the bedding and tidied the cabin. He loved all the activity and the sound of voices about the boat but seeing other people grow so familiar with *Poitín* suddenly felt uncomfortable, as if watching someone flirt with an ex-lover.

The distant island soon crawled from under its cloud-filled duvet to the vitality of another clear blue day and the harsh glare of a breakfast sun. The dark green stubble that covered the hilly eastern shore served as a reminder of the ferocity of local hurricanes and the price to be paid for such an idyllic setting.

Poitín rounded the north of the island and lost the wind in the shade of the land as she headed down the west coast to the only settlement on the island. Port Elizabeth huddled in the shelter of the surrounding hills and offered a safe anchorage to passing yachts. The red and green roofs which decorated the water's edge lay protected from the scorching sun in the shade of tall trees, while surrounding hills funnelled trade-wind gusts across the bay, causing palm trees to sway and banana plants to cast big meaty shadows along the shore.

Poitín moved across the crowded bay in her search for a space. They dropped anchor in the calm that hid inshore, waited to see how she behaved and when all appeared in order dived into the crystal clear water. They shot through the turquoise sea into the reflected sun which glared golden from sunken sand, felt a cool caress penetrate their hot dry skin and a freshness that quenched every thirsting pore. Passing through a world of liquid images, they shared in thoughts like dolphins conversing across the seas. They burst through the surface to screams of their own delight, to their gasping laughter and a wish to be heard a million miles away in the low grey skies of a northern winter.

Bequia and the other islands along the way occupied days in a way he had not known before. Nina was happy to read her way through the collection of books on board while Brigit introduced him to meditation and explored the concept of a higher self. It was the need to discover more about his soul that had driven him to sail the ocean, where he experienced that all-consuming power of love and kindness. He needed to seek out that emotion again but hoped there was another way, for he had no desire to face the abyss he was so lucky to have survived.

Twice a day they sat quietly for twenty minutes and observed whatever feelings chose to emanate from deep inside. At first he felt only frustration at the disruptive chatter of his mind but soon that passed and was replaced by an inner calm. Then one day he experienced a state of nothingness, an emotional neutral ground, without giving or taking, and sensed a special wonder in his heart as though touched by the most profound of ancient friendships while protected by the strongest of parental loves. This feeling told him he would never be alone.

Brigit spoke to him of human emotions, just like Benny had done but went on to explain how love was the definitive life force that made all living worthwhile.

'What it takes is just a little time each day to relax, shut off your mind and listen to your soul. We can encourage our emotions with openness and self-belief or we can strangle them with our fears. But one thing you can be sure of,' she said, moving to the edge of the boat. 'Your mind can drive you crazy if you don't shut it down from time to time.'

***

They entered Chatham Bay on the west side of Union Island before dark and had a sundowner while waiting on Ricardo to arrive. The main port was on the east side of the island which left the western shores devoid of habitation and the bay unaccustomed to the company of visiting boats.

Later that night, they talked as a brilliant sliver of moon rose above the island peaks casting light across the bay. Before long the deserted shore was clearly visible and a path of light etched upon the water. He fell asleep to the sound of Ricardo's haunting music and the warmth of Brigit resting against his chest.

With all the fun and excitement of sailing through the islands the girls had forgotten to check their flight details and the next morning suddenly realised that they were due to depart that same day. It was not possible for *Poitín* to get them to Grenada in time, a full day's sail away. Neither could they risk sailing around Union Island to the local airstrip. The only option that remained was to cut across the island by foot to the main village and hope to catch a flight directly to Grenada airport.

They hiked for an hour, sharing the luggage in the heat of the rising sun until a dirt track emerged through the thick scrub. They reached the top of a ridge that divided the island and paused to savour the magnificence of the view. To the northeast lay the hundreds of tiny islands that formed the Tobago Cays; precious coral jewels set into a crown of dazzling blue atop a pillar that rose from the ocean floor. The vastness of the deep Atlantic wilderness that loomed to the east of the shallow lagoons enhanced the delicate beauty of the Cays. No one spoke as they paused to share the special experience from their unique vantage point high above the sea.

They arrived at the village by two o'clock and made inquiries about inter-island flights to Grenada. With only an hour to spare before the only flight was due to depart they first cleared the boats through customs, then signed the girls off *Poitín*.

They had known each other only a week and now had to say goodbye. Addresses were swapped and promises made to keep in touch and all the while they struggled to find the words to express their sense of sharing. He hugged Nina and said something that earned him a smiled rebuke. Then he turned to Brigit and caught the sadness in her eyes before she tucked her face into his chest. He stroked her hair and whispered, 'Thanks for a very special time ... thanks for everything you've shown me.'

'I feel so much stronger for all of this,' she said. 'I knew I was right to take a chance back in Barbados. That guide never lets me down.'

Late that night he took time to write his diary:

30 JANUARY, 1991

Today I said goodbye to Brigit and Nina but feel I still have a little bit of them with me. Walking back along the dusty track to Chatham Bay was an empty experience, remembering the words, the jokes and the special moments that we had shared only a few short hours before. What is it that causes that empty feeling when saying goodbye?

I shared my boat and the joy of sailing and received so much in return. Brigit said she would never forget her Caribbean experience, nor shall I.

Ricardo and I have just eaten supper and we are agreed that *Poitín* feels empty and very quiet without our female friends. I am now back to single-handed sailing but it's only a day's sail to Grenada.

Caribbean Dance

Poitín lost the wind to the shelter of the high shore and waited by the edge of the silky calm to tow *Frédéric Chopin* into port. As the two boats proceeded across the bay, Grenada rotated towards the waiting night and the multi-coloured town that surrounded the harbour lay softened by the pastel evening light. A passing dinghy helped them find their way through a narrow channel that led from the main harbour into a protected lagoon. There they dropped anchor for the night among the other boats. The dinghy driver came by later to take up the offer of a thank-you-beer and stayed a while discussing the places to see and things to do.

Dermot was left to enjoy the local surroundings when Ricardo took *Frédéric Chopin* sailing for a few days in company with another Spanish yacht. He occupied his time alone exploring Saint George's and discovered a café by the harbour with the delicious name of 'The Nutmeg'. It was on the café terrace, from where he could observe the spectacle being acted out before him, that he loved to go each morning to linger over coffee and write letters home to family and friends.

Ricardo returned to Saint George's and decided to make a visa application in preparation for the next voyage to Venezuela. Dermot felt unsure about what to do – the thought of heading further south did not really excite him but neither did the prospect of cruising through the Caribbean alone.

Ricardo departed two days later on the understanding that if Dermot did not arrive before the end of the week, it was because he had opted to head north through the islands. He was sorry to see Ricardo leave as they had many people and places in common.

It was while he was half way up *Poitín*'s mast checking the radar reflector in preparation for the coming voyage that *Eevin* and her crew entered his mind. He knew that by staying in Barbados for so long he had foregone the opportunity to meet up in Saint Lucia and would probably not see them again until they were all back in Ireland. Maybe it was only a coincidence or maybe he sensed their presence but an hour later *Eevin* entered the narrow channel to the lagoon. His grip on the mast and the work on the reflector occupied his attention as *Eevin* moved unnoticed through the water.

'So how long have you been stuck up there?' called a voice from below.

'You git,' he shouted, startled by the strong Belfast accent. 'Are you lot trying to kill me?' he said, looking down to see *Eevin*'s fenders nudge against *Poitín* and the familiar sight of Trevor's bearded smile.

He lowered himself from the first spreader while hurling abuse for the Christmas bomb they had given him. 'You could have killed me with that thing ... I might have jumped over the side if I'd opened it on a bad day.'

Gary stepped on board. 'That's why we used full cans. We thought you might need a drink to get over the shock. Anyway, how's our Fenian mate?'

Eevin anchored in the lagoon where she stayed for the remainder of the week. He was introduced to the three new faces who had flown out to replace the previous crew and who would remain with the boat until the Virgin Islands. From there a another change of crew would see *Eevin* through the final leg of the voyage home to Belfast.

Dermot enjoyed the familiarity of *Eevin*'s all-male crew who were about his own age and had a manic sense of fun. Their enthusiasm for socialising and their commitment to alcohol was unparalleled to anything he had ever encountered. When they described the strain of living in Belfast, under the constant threat of violence and the freedom they now felt by being so far from home, he was reminded of when he was first allowed to stay out late and had tried in vain to cram every conceivable experience into that one night.

When the time finally came to depart Saint George's he decided to sail north in company with *Eevin*. Gary offered to crew on *Poitín* while they cruised through the islands and thereby help to keep pace with *Eevin*, which was bigger and faster.

Poitín arrived at the island of Saint Lucia late at night and neither Gary nor he could identify the shore. None of the navigation lights that marked the entrance to the harbour were visible and after some consideration he decided to drop all sails and drift for the remainder of the night. Gary called *Eevin* on the radio, who was already in port, to let them know that all was well but they would wait until daylight to attempt an approach.

The following morning Dermot noticed that the narrow entrance channel had been made even narrower by damage suffered in a recent gale and was glad of the decision to stay at sea overnight.

It was while in Saint Lucia that he experienced his first 'jump up', a huge street party in a residential part of town. A ten-foot high wall of speakers stood at a street corner blasting out music which set the crowd in motion. The entire neighbourhood was given over at nightfall to traders who lined the kerbs with ice boxes full of cold drinks and stalls that offered barbecued chicken, cooked on glowing embers that burned dripping fat and spewed aromatic smoke into the throbbing air. The night smells were of meat and cigarettes, of sweaty dancers and wafting smoke from local ganja. He envied the freedom of the people who packed the street in a pulsating spectacle of provocative

Caribbean dance. A human tide moved constantly through the night, drifting in a hot and dizzy flow that eventually deposited him alone on a garden wall. There he lingered a while to enjoy the silhouette of three girls dancing in the shadow of a street light and observed how they moved with a characteristic rhythm, a natural elegance.

After nearly a week of hectic socialising, the two boats departed Saint Lucia and continued north. Each island along the way possessed its own unique character and charm which never ceased to amaze him.

The two boats arrived at the southern end of Guadeloupe before sunset and by nightfall had made their way to the road bridge at the edge of the swamp. *Eevin* dropped her anchor and *Poitín* moored alongside rather than have to bother with the dinghy. The cabin lights brought insects milling about and regardless of the mosquito coils which burned throughout the night, they woke early the next morning to the sound of bird life, the hum of traffic from the overhead road and the eager work of their own scratching fingers.

After so many months of sailing in the open sea it was a refreshing change to see green plant life passing on either side of the boat. As they progressed further into the mangrove the channel began to narrow as though coming to an end. They rounded a corner where hundreds of birds were perched sunning themselves among the trees and suddenly took to the air in a magnificent display of white and pink flapping wings.

The canal eventually began to widen and their attention was drawn from the mud below to the distant power cables which straddled the swamp. Drooped from pylon to pylon, the cables posed no threat to the boats but the possibility of danger demanded attention. With all eyes squinting towards the mast tops, it was surprising that anyone noticed the small hamlet perched among the thick growth. They altered course and let the boats drift towards the far side of the lagoon. Corrugated iron sheds clung precariously to the concrete base of a huge pylon. Rusty sheets of metal, held together by bits of wood and wire, sweltered in the humidity of the afternoon heat. The smell of rotting plant life wafted through the air as did a whine from flies or power cables. A man standing by an entrance watched the boats approach but turned and stepped inside before any exchange was possible. They were intruding, viewing another world from the safety and luxury of their passing.

By late afternoon they arrived at an enormous expanse of water that separated the swamp from the open sea. Protruding rocks dotted the surface as did navigational posts marking an underwater channel that led to the far side of the lagoon. Cautiously they nudged their way from post to post until reaching an outer reef. There they found a safe place in which to anchor for the night. The salt sea air offered the opportunity to dine outside in an insect-free night where they discussed the day's events.

Probably the greatest disappointment of the entire Caribbean cruise was the Dutch island of Saint Maarten. The town of Philipsburg was completely given-over to an endless flow of tax-free shoppers that visited from cruise liners anchored in the bay. The streets were jammed with casinos and shops selling jewellery and hi-fi equipment to tourists who believed they were experiencing the Caribbean.

They departed for the British Virgin Islands, where they hoped to begin preparing the boats for the Atlantic voyage home to Ireland. The British Virgin Islands marked the end of their cruise through the Caribbean. It was late March and they had allocated three weeks in which to prepare the boats for the 4,000-mile passage home. They decided to base themselves in Roadtown, on the island of Tortola, where they could obtain any marine equipment and services they might need.

Dermot began preparations for the coming voyage, which also involved finding someone to crew on *Poitín*. For sure there were people about, seeking to cross the Atlantic but they had started their sailing careers in big yachts and had some crazy notion that small boats were not suited for ocean crossings.

He placed notices at the marinas and yacht clubs. *Poitín*, which was sometimes referred to as 'that little 28-foot boat', was advertised as a '30-foot ocean going sloop'. He played down the fact that he had crossed on his own because of a belief by some people that anyone who sailed alone did so because no one else could suffer their company. He regarded the finer detail of how *Poitín* got from Ireland to Barbados to be a little nugget of information which might be better shared when well out of sight of land. He knew that most skippers asked their crew to pay something towards their keep but in an attempt to appear generous and compensate for the fact that *Poitín*'s cabin was slightly bigger than a broom cupboard, he decided to offer free passage all the way home.

Yachties began arriving in Tortola for the Spring Regatta and he hoped that when the races finished he might succeed in coaxing someone to sail with him on *Poitín*. Trevor suggested they attend the Regatta prize-giving and pass the word around that he was looking for crew. While ordering a few drinks at the bar he began chatting to an American chap who had worked on the island for the past ten years. During the course of the conversation the American told him of a young girl who wanted to sail home to England and would be ideal crew. 'She was due to be here tonight,' he said. 'Let's hope I can find her and then it's up to you to persuade her that the boat is safe and you're a capable skipper.'

Later into the evening the American pointed to a girl on the dance floor. 'That's her over there. See that good-looking girl in the red shirt, that's Tina.' Tina was in her late twenties, with wild sun-bleached hair that flew about her face as she raged in an uncontrolled dance.

Suddenly she stopped moving, with hands and legs frozen in a rigid dance pose. Dermot looked to the others but they too were dumbfounded as they stared at Tina, who remained motionless.

The crowd continued dancing oblivious to her pose. He wondered if she might need help when unexpectedly she began dancing, as wild and excited as before. Trevor turned to him and suggested his prospective crew either required serious medical attention or was just plain weird. He looked to the American for an explanation who assured him that all was well. 'She only wants to convince some guy that she is mad. She feels sure he will leave her alone if he thinks she has some strange mental disorder.' Trevor smiled and said, 'Looks like your crew is just plain weird. Should suit you down to the ground.'

When the dancing finished the American called her over and made the introductions. Whenever Dermot tried to tell her something about *Poitín* or himself, someone from *Eevin* contradicted with a ridiculous comment. She seemed like a warm person and he liked that she made no secret of the fact that her sailing experience was limited to bigger boats than *Poitín*. He assured her it was not a problem as he wanted someone who was good company and prepared to learn how to handle *Poitín*.

Tina came to the boat the next morning, which surprised him after all the wisecracks from the previous night. He felt sure that by the time they left the sailing club she had no idea what to believe. 'At least she has a sense of humour,' he thought. They sat for a while drinking coffee in the late-morning breeze and chatted about her life in Tortola. She had crossed the Atlantic in a 65-foot yacht and spent the last three years based on the island, working on charter boats.

After the earlier night's episode, he wanted to impress on her that he was a responsible sailor and not some drunken lunatic who would end her days in the middle of the ocean. He began by describing the layout of the boat and then explained the various pieces of equipment on board, paying special attention to safety and survival gear. 'Unlike large yachts,' he explained, '*Poitín* doesn't have a long-range radio and once we are out of sight of land, that's it – we'll be on our own. The boat has to be fully self-contained because the nearest supplies or help of any kind could be thousands of miles away.'

'I think that covers everything,' he said, feeling he had expressed himself well and had recovered some ground from the night before. 'Any questions?'

She thought for a moment and then asked, 'Will we have any games to play?'

'Holy shit,' he thought, 'is that all she is concerned with? She cannot be serious?' There was silence as Tina watched his anxiety grow. 'Joke!' she said, smiling triumphantly. 'That's for last night.'

He felt Tina would be ideal for the voyage. She had crossed an ocean before and it was obvious her lack of small boat experience would not pose a problem. She had a great sense of humour, of that there was no doubt, but best of all she appeared to be strong willed and responsible. She knew there was a certain amount of danger involved but she was relying on him as skipper and owner to ensure the boat was fully prepared for whatever lay ahead. Before leaving she did, however, ask to see the boat's papers and he wondered if it was another joke or if she really wanted to check who owned *Poitín*.

When first preparing to leave Arklow, he had taken reasonable precautions and thought that if anything happened to him it was then simply a case of bad luck. Now things were different. He had acquired a new appreciation for living and a desire to see his family again. No longer was he prepared to take unnecessary risks with life but, more importantly, he was about to take responsibility for another person.

He moved *Poitín* to a berth in the marina and began work for the Atlantic crossing. They would be sailing north into higher latitudes and could expect all types of weather, especially between the Azores and Ireland.

With the help of Trevor and Gary, every inch of rigging was checked, from the masthead to the deck. Fittings which showed the slightest sign of metal fatigue were replaced. A thorough inspection was made of the entire electrical system. Additional grab-handles were fitted in the main cabin to make life a little safer and more comfortable. *Poitín* was hauled out of the water for cleaning and anti-fouling. For some unknown reason he felt that same uneasiness about the rudder that had caused him to have it rebuilt in Dublin and so he removed it once again for quick inspection.

***

On Sunday, with only three days left and a few minor jobs remaining, they took time to celebrate *Eevin*'s twenty-first year. Tina was too busy sorting out her personal affairs to join them but they both accepted that a day's sailing across the bay was insufficient time to discover how they would get along.

***

Tuesday morning arrived with all the usual tension and excitement of a departure day. It was three months since they had done any serious sailing and they were anxious about heading out into the Atlantic again. They hoped to arrive in Ireland by early June, but with nearly 4,000 miles of ocean to cross and latitudes as high as 55^0 degrees north, they were prepared for all conditions.

Tina arrived, wheeling a trolley heaped with personal belongings. At first he laughed, suspecting it was another prank but soon realised she was serious. They went through each bag identifying what was really necessary and what could be sent on later.

At 13:00 he started the engine on *Poitín*, made a few last checks and with an encouraging calmness, for his stomach trembled out of control, cast off the shore lines. Tina waved to friends who had come to see her off as *Poitín* reversed out of the berth, turned to port and headed for the open sea.

Into the Madness

Dermot woke to the sound of Van the Man's haunting music and the smell of freshly-baked bread wafting through the cabin. Without looking outside he could tell conditions had improved simply by the sound of Tina singing. She made no secret of the fact that she had not a single musical note in her body and only ever sang when happy and alone. As *Poitín* rolled on the Atlantic swell he caught glimpses of the high clouds that brought Tina joy. The rain and gusting wind which had hounded *Poitín* for the past four days were no longer to be seen. In their place was a gentle overcast sky and a wind that blew soft and cool from the west.

He moved his head slightly on the pillow to watch the shifting light dance among the shadows and saw Tina outside. She sat wedged into a corner with what looked like a writing pad against her knees and from the movement of her hand realised she had been sketching his sleeping form. She greeted his look with a smile. The slow two week passage to Bermuda had given them ample time to discover how much they enjoyed each other's company. The intimate confines of life on board *Poitín* quickly dispensed with character acting and uncovered their real personalities. After much persuasion, Tina held up the pad for him to see. The quality of her work impressed him and he told her so.

The improvement in the weather was celebrated with a gin and tonic but he forgot to listen to the weather forecast. When the time came for supper he offered to cook. Throughout the two hours needed to prepare the meal she taunted and questioned his cooking techniques. But within half an hour of eating, her enthusiasm expired and she crawled into bed leaving him to the first watch of the night.

Having slept for most of the afternoon he was content to listen to music on the Walkman and watch another night saunter across the sky. *Poitín* moved along at a steady three knots, riding the six-foot swell with a comfortable roll. He could have hoisted more sail to improve their progress, but since leaving Bermuda they had clocked up 1,000 miles and with the same distance remaining, he felt a comfortable night was far more important. In return for having allowed him to sleep for so long during the day he waited until midnight before calling her.

He loved this period, this change of watch, when after hours in bed, time was needed to wake and he would put the kettle on for tea and they would talk a while. Remembering the long empty nights spent sailing alone, he cherished more than ever the comfort of her voice. Her female tones were soft and lilting and her words a gentle lullaby on which to rest his mind.

The enjoyment of the moment gave way to sleep and like bedclothes pulled across a jaded child to end another day, heavy lids caressed his sleepy eyes. And this was how the night passed, like most nights, reversing roles on every shift until dawn appeared and their appetites for sleep turned to food.

Tina prepared a big breakfast of tinned sausages, eggs and hash browns while he fiddled with the radio. A weather forecast warned of a low-pressure system to the north with winds ranging from 25 to 40 knots. He estimated they had twelve hours of pleasant weather before riding out another blow.

In preparation for the pending gale, Tina cooked a pot of stew and began storing all loose items in lockers. He ran the engine for an hour to charge up the batteries and anything on deck which could not go below was secured with extra lines. Once all the preparations were completed, it was simply a matter of enjoying, as best they could, the lively sailing until the gale arrived.

By midnight the seas had begun to build, well in advance of the wind speed. From the weather forecast he expected waves of around fifteen feet high but they were already close to that and the wind had not yet reached gale force. He felt angry with the unseasonal weather.

He was about to check outside when the silence of the cabin was broken by the sound of a voice on the VHF radio. 'Merchant vessel, merchant vessel, this is yacht *Eevin* approximately five miles off your port bow, do you see us, over.'

Tina woke, confused by the words that had entered her sleeping world. 'Was I dreaming or did I just hear Trevor on the radio?' They waited a few minutes for the ship's reply but when none was heard he called to let them know that *Poitín* was nearby. They chatted for some time, amazed at how they had crossed paths after nearly 1,000 miles of sailing. The two boats had departed Bermuda seven days ago but had all lost contact within 24 hours. Before signing off for the night they agreed on a compass course by which to sail and make VHF contact in the morning.

The barometer fell rapidly throughout the night while wind and waves grew in strength. By early morning they were once again in the teeth of a gale. While he discussed the worsening weather with Trevor, a wave hit *Poitín* square on the stern with ferocious power that threw her broadside to the advancing waves. Tina continued the radio call while he donned his harness and struggled outside to put the boat back on course.

Poitín felt strange. He adjusted the self-steering but she did not respond. He untied the tiller and pulled it to port but nothing happened. He jerked the tiller frantically from side to side and again there was nothing. Panic gripped his mind at the realisation that there was no resistance to the water.

'No, God, please no, not this, oh Jesus Christ, not a broken rudder, please God ... no.' Fear surged through his body as though the same demon wave which snapped the rudder now burst through him driving twisted innards towards his mouth. He heaved but only winded breath passed his lips. He knelt in the cockpit trying desperately to grasp the reality of the situation. He checked and re-checked the tiller but each time the horror of their predicament drove the stark realisation through his mind – north-Atlantic-broken-rudder-worsening-gale.

Breaking waves pounded *Poitín* mercilessly, throwing her about like a rag doll in the jaws of a raving dog. He crawled back to the safety of the cabin. Tina saw his fear. Afraid to ask what could have caused such terror, she waited. He wiped the water from his face and pummelled the heel of his palms into his eyes as he explained.

Tina was speechless. She held the microphone to her mouth as a voice crackled from the radio, 'Are you still there, Tina?'

She passed the microphone, her gaze frozen on his face. He steadied himself for a moment. 'Trevor ... we're in serious trouble here ... we have no steering.'

The words filled the radio and travelled across the sea where such things were feared.

'Say again Dermot.'

'Our rudder is broken, we have no steering.'

Trevor agreed it was critical that *Eevin* locate *Poitín* and stand by should they need to be rescued. *Poitín*'s electronic navigator gave her exact geographical location but Trevor, who relied on a sextant, had not taken an accurate sun sight in days. The strength of the radio signal suggested the boats were within five miles of each other but there was no way of knowing from which direction it came. They called to any ships which might be in the area but heard nothing. *Eevin* fired off a white flare at an agreed time while Tina and he scanned the horizon but they failed to see anything. The flares would work better at night but they could not risk waiting that long. There was no way of knowing how long *Poitín* would survive the pounding waves.

When all seemed lost he noticed an unusual opening in the clouds to the north. A possibility crossed his mind and he called *Eevin* to describe what he saw. As soon as the cloud formation was confirmed they took compass bearings relative to their positions. From this information *Eevin* began searching for *Poitín*, calling every fifteen minutes to check on the strength of the radio signal.

***

Poitín lay broadside in the water, the waves crashing into her as they rushed past. It was obvious some form of emergency steering had to be rigged to gain control but the smallest task demanded major effort. Hours of holding on to avoid being thrown across the boat were exhausting.

They crawled outside and made their way to the stern. He squeezed under the safety rail until his body hung upside down above the water, with Tina sitting on the backs of his legs. From what he could see the rudder was intact but the shaft appeared to have broken inside the rudder blade. All that was required was to devise a way to snag the blade so that it could be held in place. Using a piece of nylon netting attached to two lengths of rope, he hoped they could somehow catch the pointed edge of the rudder and secure the lines.

The procedure demanded they both squeeze under the safety rail, exposing them to the full force of the sea. Tina lowered one of the ropes while he tried to direct the net with the boat hook. Their combined weight, hanging so far aft, affected the balance of the boat. A wave charged at *Poitín* and broke across the stern. His safety harnesses tightened against the force that tried to sweep him overboard. The cold water drove the air from his nose and flooded through the neck of his jacket. He tried to rise against the sudden weight but could not move and held his breath until his lungs were about to burst. He thought of Tina being subjected to the same force and hoped she had not been washed overboard. The wave swept towards the bow. *Poitín's* stern burst through the surface and rose high above the churning foam, leaving the rudder exposed to the clear light of day. Gasping for breath, desperate to fill their lungs they coughed and choked as they shimmied back into the relative safety of the cockpit.

Their effort seemed futile and dangerous but Tina insisted they had come very close to succeeding and should continue. Two hours of struggle and countless drenchings passed before the rudder was finaly snagged and tied in a centre position. He reset the self-steering and very slowly *Poitín* came back on course with her stern square to the waves.

Eevin had failed to locate *Poitín* by late afternoon. With day-light waning they agreed to fire another flare. Once again Tina and he crawled outside into the madness of the gale and stood clasping the mast as they searched the horizon. *Poitín* rode high on the back of a passing wave and Dermot caught sight of the white light that rose into the gray clouds to the west. They called *Eevin* on the radio and gave a compass bearing by which to steer.

Three hours after sighting the flare, *Eevin* was standing by, her masthead light clearly visible a quarter of a mile off their port bow. It was impossible for *Eevin* to get near to *Poitín* in the heaving seas but she was close enough to help if Tina and he found it necessary to abandon the boat. He called Trevor on the radio to discuss the procedure for launching the life raft and being picked up by *Eevin*.

The seas increased in size and *Poitín* took a hammering like nothing she had ever known. He tried reassuring Tina, and in doing so himself, that the situation was not quite as bad at it appeared. She returned the gesture by agreeing with his assess-ment but could see they were dangerously close to the edge.

Eevin had sufficient crew to keep watch throughout the

night and agreed to call on the VHF if any ships appeared. With nothing more to be done except wait and hope, Tina threw some cushions on the floor and wedged herself into what she regarded as the most comfortable berth in a gale. He climbed into the bunk and fell into a deep sleep, exhausted from the day's events. Tina lay awake, unable to sleep for the sound of the waves crashing against the hull and the violent motion that ensured endless rubbing of bones against skin.

By morning, a strong wind continued to blow, but the seas had fallen in size. The barometer began rising and it appeared the worst was over. Conditions improved throughout the day and by evening the wind had decreased to 25 knots and the waves to a manageable size. *Poitín* responded well to the storm-jib and triple reefed mainsail and by balancing the sails with the self-steering they found it possible to set a course for the Azores.

Tina and he were pleased with *Poitín's* progress but above all else, they were thankful for having come through an incredibly dangerous situation. Neither of them knew how *Poitín* had succeeded in riding out the gale and they speculated on whether she could have survived much worse.

It was obvious that with the proper balance of sails, *Poitín* was capable of handling herself. Although her progress was slow, *Eevin* stayed patiently by for the remainder of the week, spilling wind from her sails so as not to pull too far ahead. They lost sight of Eevin during a night of heavy rain and by morning, *Poitín* once again had the ocean to herself.

Dermot called Tina at 08:30 and greeted her with the news that the forecast was for light fifteen-knot winds. The sky had cleared and the morning sun streamed into the cabin as *Poitín* slowly crawled along. He sat with Tina in the cockpit for a while discussing the possibility of good weather prevailing until they reached the Azores. They were more than halfway there, with 800 miles remaining, but at *Poitín's* slow rate of sailing it could take up to two weeks. The longer *Poitín* remained at sea, the

greater the chance of encountering bad weather. The only con-
solation was that each day brought them closer to the
favourable weather of the high-pressure system normally associated with the Azores. 'Surely the gales of the past ten days
have cleared the air,' he thought and began persuading Tina
likewise.

He left Tina on watch and climbed into bed for a few hours
sleep after breakfast. Before closing his eyes he glanced through
the hatch and thought how good it felt to see her bop to the
music, especially when he remembered the events of the previous gale. Tina looked happy and relaxed in the glorious sunshine but above all, she was safe. He sensed a new energy from
her as though having gained in strength from their survival. He
wished to breath the power of her enthusiasm but instead felt
an exhausted sigh emanate from every limb, as though having
held his breath since being swamped in the gale.

Dermot slept solidly for four hours and was eventually
coaxed from bed by the smell of coffee. Outside he scooped the
passing sea in a bucket and splashed the cold freshness on his
face. He plunged his head into the ocean pail and, like a dripping dog upon a shore, shook off any remaining doom.

The tranquil weather continued for the next few days. They
listened anxiously to the radio each morning and breathed a
sigh of relief with every favourable forecast. They played board
games, listened to music and finished each day with a celebratory gin and tonic. On Tuesday, Tina began to feel low as emotional and physical exhaustion caught up with her. She stayed
in bed sleeping until mid afternoon and he moved quietly about
the boat. She had supported him when he was down and now
needed to unwind.

While she slept, he spent some time pondering the daily
plots on the chart which showed how painfully slow *Poitín* progressed towards her destination. Balancing the sails in such a
way as to steer *Poitín* meant she was underpowered and could
average less than half her normal speed. In the five days since

the rudder had broken only 250 miles had been covered. The self-steering performed admirably in moderate winds, but he could not help wondering what would happen if they ran into more bad weather.

Dermot began sketching a makeshift steering system which involved securing a sling, made from rigging wire and anchor chain, around the rudder with two ropes connected to either side. The spinnaker pole was to be lashed across the cockpit, with pulley blocks shackled to both ends, for the purpose of passing the rudder ropes inboard. The ropes were to be tied to the tiller which could then serve to pull the rudder from side to side. There was no reason why it would not work but, for the moment, *Poitín* moved along nicely and he decided not to upset the status quo.

The following morning *Poitín* sat becalmed on the ocean while they listened to the radio for the weather forecast. Tina and he froze in disbelief with the news that a 'complex storm' was on the way. It was forecast to cover an area of 900 square miles, bringing with it winds of up to 60 knots and waves the height of *Poitín*'s mast.

After the initial shock and a feeling of helplessness had subsided, they agreed something had to be done. He sketched the jury-rigged steering system in detail and explained it to Tina, who was of the opinion that it made sense and was worth trying.

Using a mask and snorkel he climbed over the stern. Tina kept watch while he vanished under the boat for far longer than she cared to imagine.

Within fifteen minutes he succeeded in fitting the harness around the rudder. He took a break with a cup of tea and while they discussed what next to do, a cargo ship appeared on the horizon. Tina succeeded in raising the captain on the VHF who confirmed the weather forecast and added, 'As a disabled boat you are in a very dangerous position. I will cut my engines and drift towards you which should give you about fifteen minutes to decide if you want to come with us.'

The ship loomed closer with only a microsecond of a life-time in which to make up their minds. 'Either we stay with *Poitín* and take our chances, or we abandon her,' he said. 'If we get this wrong it might very well be the end for us.'

As he spoke he saw himself standing onboard the ship watching *Poitín* slowly sink into the depths of the Atlantic. He saw his family's grief should he not return and felt his own upset for failing to complete the voyage. He saw the terror of the pending gale and felt an overpowering appreciation of his life. He saw for the first time how all things in life are evenly balanced. How with loved-ones comes the fear of their loss, with the sweet taste of success comes the fear of failure and with the gift of living comes the fear of death.

Once again he forced his mind to focus on the decision. 'I'm afraid. Too afraid to decide for both of us,' he thought. 'I just want to be safe, that's all. I want Tina to be safe. I don't know if I have the strength to face another gale. We should go with the ship. Big ship. Big safe ship, with warm cabins and showers and windows high above the sea. And from those windows we could view the storm. Oh bollocks to this storm, it could kill us both.'

Before deciding on which course of action to take, they agreed to first complete the repairs to the rudder. With a new sense of urgency he returned to the water. In a few minutes he succeeded in attaching the two steering lines to the harness and handed them to Tina. She then passed them through the pulleys on either end of the spinnaker pole and secured them to the tiller. She moved the tiller, which pulled on the ropes, which swung the rudder without any obstruction. He clambered back on board, shivering from the cold and was greeted with Tina's enthusiasm. 'We have steering? We can steer the boat, right? We'll be OK?'

She needed to hear his assessment of the situation but he was reluctant to persuade her one way or the other. He could specu-late as to how the makeshift steering would weather the storm but the last thing he wanted was to gamble with Tina's safety.

Tina felt sure the rougher conditions which lay ahead would be outweighed by the fact that *Poitín* now had steering. '*Poitín* looked after us before,' she said, appearing strong and brave. 'Surely it's now up to us to return the favour. I can't imagine leaving her, it would be like walking away from part of myself. How must you feel? We owe it to ourselves and to *Poitín* to complete the voyage. I feel sure we will be OK.'

Deep down, he knew the safest thing to do was accept the captain's offer but he felt *Poitín* was capable of seeing them through. 'Assuming the steering holds,' he thought. He felt ashamed of his fear in the face of Tina's conviction but was relieved by her committment to continue. He hugged her and felt as men sometimes do in the arms of a woman when faced with desperate times. The urge to climb inside her and curl up in her womb and feel safe once more where the world could no longer find him.

Tina called the captain while Dermot changed into dry clothes and explained that they had managed to rig emergency steering which was good enough to survive the storm. The captain wished them luck and suggested utilising the next twelve hours before the storm arrived to get as far south as possible. 'Sixty miles will not make a huge difference,' he thought. 'But it might help a little.' He knew the importance of morale and the need to feel that something was being done to improve their chances of survival.

Poitín's engine spluttered to a halt. He checked the fuel and discovered it contained sea water. Frantically he began pulling gear from the aft locker and crawled inside from where he could access the diesel tank. Tina tried to calm him, calling words of reason through the open hatch but his rage was beyond control. He loosened the metal plug in the bottom of the tank and grunted arguments as to why this was happening to him.

Dermot drained the water until clean diesel appeared and then began tightening the plug. On the final turn the spanner gave way and his knuckles grazed against the roughness of the hull leaving skin and blood imbedded in the cracks. Diesel gushed over his hand into the bilge. 'You idiot, what are you doing ... oh fuck you God, why this now?' He stuck his finger in the hole and felt his anger give way to survival. Realising he had better control his temper if they were to stand any chance of making it through the next two days, he slowly pulled himself together.

The eerie calm which hung over them all morning was at last broken. A gentle wind began to blow and they hoisted sails to help the engine drive *Poitín* on. It was hard to imagine that the tiny ripples which creased the surface of their millpond would grow in size as the day progressed. He wondered how many hours would pass before those same ripples towered overhead. Soon the blue skies gave way to intimidating grey clouds and as the wind increased they changed sails but not until absolutely necessary.

By nightfall *Poitín*'s sail area was reduced to triple-reefed main and a small storm jib. She surfed down the ever-increasing seas as if she too was eager to get as far as possible from the approaching storm. The emergency steering began vibrating with the speed and there was no other choice but to slow the boat down and prepare to ride out the gale where they were.

The waves grew steadily throughout the night but they were rounded and regular which made it easier for *Poitín* to cope. Conditions below were surprisingly comfortable and bore no relationship to the howling wind or the falling barometer. Tina and he knew they could expect a more serious gale but it was the waiting they found hardest. If the weather forecast proved correct, the approaching storm would be worse than anything he had ever encountered. He tried not to think of the steering giving way again.

By early morning the millpond of yesterday resembled a giant prehistoric creature which ranted and raved and drove *Poitín* uncontrollably down the face of the waves. The combination of triple-reefed mainsail and storm jib offered too much resistance to the crazed wind. They were left with no alternative but to venture into the waning night to douse the remaining sails.

Outside conditions were wild. Every drop of water flew through the air like tiny missiles, making it impossible to look in the direction of the wind. Without any deck lights, his body functioned in the reality of shackles twisted, hanks removed and halyards worked, just like it had done thousands of times before. But his mind remained detached, viewing the situation from afar as if too afraid to join him in the storm. He struggled with the sail that fought to be free of *Poitín* as though alerted to doom and preferring to take its chances on the wind.

His mouth blabbered words of support while maintaining a grip on the boat. 'Everything is OK, Dermot. It's rough but the boat is safe, at this moment the boat is safe, the boat is safe. Just help her survive.'

The waves continued to build in size and by daybreak they were experiencing the roughest conditions he had ever seen. Walls of water charged at *Poitín*. With only her mast and rigging to catch the wind, she was driven across the surface and seemed to cope until a rogue wave, which was steeper and faster than the norm, crashed against her hull. Her tiny shape stalled in a deep trough and waited in hope of mercy. The following wave ripped across the deck, rolling *Poitín* on her side. Tina sat clasping the chart table as *Poitín* fell from the top of the wave. He watched her face distort with fear while they waited for what seemed like an eternity for *Poitín* to crash to a halt. Water poured through the ventilator. *Poitín* slowly righted herself. Without any apparent damage she lay broadside to the seas once again. Something had to be done to ensure that she had some chance of riding out the gale.

'We're moving too slow,' he said, knowing only too well that he was committing them both to going outside. 'We need to get control of the boat if she is to survive these waves. We need to hoist some sail, not as much as before.' What he suggested involved removing the final reef of the mainsail from the mast and wrapping it around the boom until only a fraction remained. Tina agreed it was worth trying without any apparent reluctance to leave the safety of the cabin.

Outside, their world had gone berserk. Huge bodies of water, towering above, charged at the most incredible speeds. Low black clouds raced across the sky. They watched in amazement as *Poitín* miraculously rode the waves but occasionally, green, folding crests smashed into her, shaking her tiny frame from stem to stern. Nothing could have prepared them for the sense of power and violence which filled the air. The sea was oblivious to their presence. *Poitín* somehow related to the madness like a punch-crazed fighter struggling to survive until the final bell. She was made to weave and duck her giant opponent but could not go on indefinitely. He sensed her begging for help.

They crawled onto the coach roof, clinging to the grab rails and called to each other above the deafening noise to warn of approaching waves. Grasping the boom, they slowly removed the sail from the mast and began the long process of rolling it around the boom. The procedure seemed to take forever as each roll of the sail was interrupted by violent gusts of wind which sought to fill the cloth and rip it from their grasp.

With the shortened sail prepared, Tina returned to the cockpit to control the sheet while he hauled on the halyard. As the sail bellied with wind, Tina eased out the boom and *Poitín* began moving ahead at a steady speed. Dermot crawled back to the cockpit and altered course so that *Poitín* worked with the waves rather than took them on the beam. Tina then held the course using the tiller while he set the self-steering. They waited to see how *Poitín* reacted. The difference was impressive – she rode down the face of the waves leaving the green folding tops to break astern. With the tiller tied in place, they left the self-steering to sail the boat.

The day passed slowly. They listened to the radio and sometimes talked but mostly they thought their private thoughts. He tried to imagine the force that controlled the world in which they struggled to survive. He remembered how Marlo had said that to experience the newborn is to know life's force. 'Forget about the hereafter, contacting the dead and tunnels of light. The wonder of life cannot be described with the spoken word or painted by the eye or touched by the feeling hand. These are things we use to experience this world. The power of life is an emotion and can only be felt by that special place deep within you. We know when we are in love, without any need of proof or scientific explanation, or even the opinion of another. We simply feel the burning inside and know.

'Some day you will realise you have enough power and love to handle any problems you choose to experience in this life. Every time you ask for help from the supernatural rather than rely on the power within, you pass responsibility for your world. If you struggle with a problem and fail, can you then say, well, it was God's will, Inch Allah?'

Dermot considered Marlo's words. Could it be he was insulting God each time he sought help? To implore some imagined power far off in the heavens while ignoring his own personal gift of life seemed ridiculous. There in mid-Atlantic, in the depths of the storm, he turned within for the strength to survive and hoped he was not about to invoke the wrath of sacrilege.

With eyes closed he tried to meditate just like Brigit had shown him. He focused on the breath that guaranteed his life and listened until he came under the spell of its slow steady rhythm. A point of calm deep within began to glow and drew him from the world he feared. He felt touched by the very same love which had lifted him from the pit of despair when alone. It cupped the water around *Poitín* in a pool of emotion and protected her from the waves. Holding this experience, not as an image in his mind but as the strength of soul, he confronted the storm with belief in the moment.

The barometer stopped falling by late afternoon but outside the gale showed no sign of abating. The evening weather forecast indicated that the storm would move away in a north-east direction. They could not expect any improvement in the conditions for the next twelve hours but at least there was no longer any need to worry about the weather worsening. The uncomfortable conditions seemed bearable once they knew the worst was over.

By early morning on the last Friday in May, the barometer began to rise and the wind eased back a few knots. They both breathed a sigh of relief at having come through safely. The whole episode had left him feeling totally exhausted. He was drained of every last ounce of energy and climbed into bed after breakfast. Tina was delighted with the prospect of better weather and offered to stay on watch all morning while he slept.

As the days progressed the weather improved and life on board returned to normal. He took advantage of the calmer conditions to hoist more sail and push *Poitín* to her limit. On Sunday morning when Tina came on watch she was greeted with grey skies and rain. He assured her the forecast made no mention of bad weather but she was not impressed by what she saw.

The grey clouds passed and *Poitín* was returned to perfect sailing conditions. Tina was soon back to normal and they both refreshed their enthusiasm for the remainder of the passage. They never failed to listen to the weather forecast and greeted each day's good news with cheers and laughter and gratitude. *Poitín* romped along, clocking up nearly 100 miles per day. He considered getting in the water to check the makeshift steering but it had survived the storm. He presumed it would hold until they reached the Azores.

Dolphins came and played alongside *Poitín* one afternoon. Tina cheered and shouted as each shining body broke the surface. Appearing to sense her joy they responded by staying with *Poitín* for a while. As they played and performed their tricks at random, sometimes catapulting clear of the water, Tina tried in vain to catch them on camera but there was no way of telling where they would next appear.

Each day they moved closer to their destination and felt increasingly confident of getting into port safely once *Poitín* was under the influence of the Azores' high-pressure system.

Near the end of his watch on the morning of the first Friday in June he sighted a dark patch of cloud on the horizon. When Tina came on watch he greeted her with the news that the weather forecast was favourable and the Azores lay on the horizon. At long last they could breathe a sigh of relief and with only ten hours of sailing before arriving in port they could say for definite that *Poitín* was out of danger.

The island of Faial gradually rose above the horizon and was transformed from a dark cloudy patch to a beautiful green oasis on the vastness of the Atlantic ocean. Fields and houses began to take shape and by mid-afternoon *Poitín* was proudly making her approach to the port of Horta.

Soul Upon the Sea

Dermot imagined the island to be a great protectorate whose enormous stone piers embraced voyagers with welcoming arms. Tina rushed to the foredeck for a clearer view of the new surroundings and with one hand on the forestay began dancing excitedly at what she saw. Dermot jumped onto the cockpit seat and joined in the celebration. 'We made it!' he shouted. 'We're here Tina, we're safe.'

The further *Poitín* moved across the harbour the more protected they felt, which increased the strength of their exhilaration. No one appeared to take any notice as the new arrival passed on the sheltered water.

With the spinnaker pole lashed across the stern, manoeuvring alongside the other boats at the customs quay proved difficult. They nudged *Poitín* into place and breathed a final sigh of relief. It was while securing shore lines that they heard people shouting, and looked to see the crews of *Eevin* and *Halcyon* bounding down the quay. Tina hurried across the neighbouring boats to join them and was greeted with kisses and hugs which brought tears to her eyes. They called to Dermot but he felt reluctant to leave *Poitín*.

Dermot was overcome with emotion, not of joy or sadness, nor anger or calm but a feeling of strength about his person. This was real power – self-belief contained within the spirit of an individual, without the need to expose another's weakness or declare itself from atop a pyramid of might. But he knew that once he stepped from the arena of boat and sea this power would no longer reign supreme and would battle for survival amid the insecurities of daily life. Much had happened in three weeks but little had altered in appearance. Words were lost to him except for 'Go on ahead, I'll catch up with you in a few minutes.'

How could he leave *Poitín*? She had given more than he had ever imagined possible and now deserved to share in the celebrations. He glanced at the makeshift steering with its frayed rope-ends and salt-encrusted blocks and marvelled at the violence she had endured. As she rested peacefully beside the other boats he felt a pang of pride and said a prayer to the god of sea and craft. Before leaving he kissed the coach roof and whispered his appreciation. 'Thank you *Poitín*, thanks for my life.'

Later that evening they made their way through the cobbled streets to Pete's Café which overlooked the harbour. The bar was popular with visiting boat crews and for many, Horta was the last port of call before returning home.

They stayed in Horta for two weeks, relaxing after their ordeal and making repairs. He borrowed diving gear and removed the rudder without the need to slip *Poitín* at the local boatyard. Once the blade was cut open it was possible to see where the strips of stainless steel, which were welded to the shaft, had broken from the force of the wave. He had sensed a problem with the steering back in Arklow when preparing *Poitín* and removed the rudder for inspection. 'How could it have broken?' he thought. 'No, not how, but why?'

In the quiet of the evening when Tina had gone ashore Dermot committed the confusion of the day to his diary:

I removed the rudder today and the problem appears to be either a simple case of metal fatigue or *Poitín* was not designed for the rigours of ocean sailing. No, I can't say that about her. *Poitín* has performed brilliantly over thousands of miles, one lousy mishap is not going to start me slagging her off.

While I was working today I kept thinking about Brigit's advice on intuition and how we should always heed those little whispers in the back of our minds. She believes that they are words from a spiritual loved one who looks after us for our lifetime. I obviously heard something when I removed the rudder in Arklow, even though I wasn't aware of it at the time. But what I don't understand is that I consciously heeded my intuition when I sensed the need to check the rudder in Tortola and I removed it again for inspection.

Now that I think of it, I had the opportunity to see the inside of the rudder in Dublin but didn't make the time and then I felt uncomfortable about it afterwards. I wonder now if it was not just by chance that whenever I opened a sailing book or magazine in Tortola I invariably happened upon an article on emergency steering. What about that piece of wire and the scrap of chain which I very nearly tossed out, but didn't? And that length of rope that I spliced a loop on either end because I had a notion it would be of use some-day. Jesus, every piece of the emergency steering was wait-ing to be used, even those two oversized blocks that I used on either end of the spinnaker pole – they were sitting in the shed at home for years. I don't even remember putting them onboard. What's going on here?

He flicked back through his diary to when Brigit was on board and then to La Coruña.

I've had some great chats with Benny. Some of what he believes is fascinating but some of it is over the top. That story he told me yesterday about spirits in heaven selecting their friends and enemies really has me thinking. He believes that each of us here on earth has a spiritual friend who watches over us, which is much the same as the concept of a guardian angel that I was brought up with. Except he believes that when we die we will have to return the favour and look after someone here on earth. I just can't imagine myself as someone's angel. Anyway, he told me to listen for advice in the form of an inner voice if I wanted to know the right thing to do in life. If I remember correctly he said, 'Your emotions shout the loudest but your spirit is the clearest of whispers. You won't always like what it says but it's always right.'

Fortunately Horta had a choice of good marine workshops and Dermot had no difficulty in obtaining the materials to make the necessary repairs. While he worked on the rudder, Tina emptied the lockers which were damp from the weeks of bad weather and rinsed the contents in fresh water. *Poitín* began taking shape for another passage and the demands of the ocean returned to fill his mind.

It was in Bermuda Dermot last checked the rigging. A voice reminded him that was 2,000 miles ago and the heavy weather might have taken its toll. He didn't hear the voice but felt the same uneasiness that had first caused him to remove the rudder in Arklow. Halfway up the mast he discovered broken rivets on the top spreader and heard the echo of the voice that had spoken strong and clear. He paused for a moment and thought, 'Is that how it sounds, like a distant echo, not even that, more a feeling, which could easily go unnoticed?'

Eevin had delayed her departure to help *Poitín* make repairs. On Monday morning *Eevin* said goodbye as she set out on the last 1,000 miles home to Ireland. He felt strange standing on the quay watching her leave without *Poitín*. The two boats had shared thousands of miles together and a multitude of experiences. The Azores marked the final stage of the Atlantic cruise from where each boat would go their separate ways.

Tina and he were eager to get sailing but were apprehensive about heading out into the precarious weather of the northern latitudes. It was late morning by the time they said goodbye to their remaining friends. As was the custom for boats departing on an ocean passage, *Poitín* received a blast of horns as she made her way through the marina. All too soon the hooting faded and *Poitín* gingerly poked her nose out into the Atlantic once more.

Luck saw a fresh south-west breeze embrace *Poitín* and carry her from Faial at a steady five knots. They took it as a good omen for the passage ahead that the Azores high pressure system, which often resulted in very little wind, was not to be found. *Poitín* romped along, see-sawing her way over the Atlantic swell which gradually increased the further she moved from the shelter of land. By the time the sun had laid its head on the smooth horizon, Faial was well astern and the tiny island of Graciosa was ten miles to starboard. The vastness of the waiting ocean teased with memories of *Poitín*'s survival during the bad weather. He found it difficult to relax and occupied the time, which anxiety sought to fill, by checking the navigation.

Gradually, the daily routine of sleeping and eating, of cooking and sailing, took control of their lives. The weather was noticeably colder and much of the time off watch was spent below in the comfort of the cabin. On Friday, their third day at sea, while he was below reading, Tina began calling to a dolphin. He listened with amusement to her 'coo cooo, coo cooo' song which she performed to the sound of clapping hands. He considered joining in the fun but before he could do so she put her head through the open hatch and said, 'Dermot, there is a horrible smell of rotten fish.'

'I don't get it,' he said, sniffing the air.

'Not in there silly, out here, from the dolphin.'

He went outside into the cool of the afternoon but could

smell nothing unusual. They scanned the rippled sea, waiting for the dolphin to return. Suddenly a large black fin broke through the surface not far from *Poitín*, spraying water high into the air. Below the surface the enormous body of a black and white killer whale passed close to *Poitín*'s stern. The following wind carried the decending vapours across the cockpit, coating them in the foul exhalation.

The whale appeared curious and circled continuously as *Poitín* sailed along at a steady pace. There was no disputing the creature's beauty but the immense size and strength posed a danger to the boat. After a short while the whale disappeared into the depths and as the minutes ticked by they relaxed and assumed it had continued on its way.

The sea erupted on the port side. This time the whale headed straight towards *Poitín*, moving faster than before. In the split-second it took the fin to reach the boat, they grabbed the safety rail and watched in terror as it darted under the bow. Dermot braced for the violent collision which would see the keel ripped from the hull and *Poitín* vanish in a matter of seconds. But the moment for impact passed and the whale surfaced on the other side. It then charged through the water at an incredible speed, as if spurred into action for some reason. Dermot had read of killer whales inadvertantly sinking yachts with an flick of a fin when playful or sexually aroused. But they were also known to make deliberate attacks without any provocation.

It was obvious they could not sit tight and simply hope it would go away – something had to be done. Tina quickly spilled the wind from the sails while he started the engine, hoping the sound of the exhaust and the lack of movement through the water would cause the whale to lose interest. Tina scanned the surface to port and he kept watch to starboard, anxiously hoping it would not appear. Twenty minutes passed without a sighting. Presuming they were safe, they began sailing again with the engine running.

The weather improved by Sunday without turning nasty and they slipped into the week occupying the days in the usual way. For the first time they chatted about returning home and what direction their lives might take. They looked forward to seeing family and friends but agreed it was hard to imagine a world beyond *Poitín*.

On Wednesday, with 500 miles to go, the BBC weather forecast came through loud and clear on channel four. It was the first forecast since leaving the Azores and knowing what to expect for the days ahead delighted them. Dermot grew increasingly excited at the prospect of returning home after nearly 12,000 miles sailing. He became obsessive about safety on board, afraid something might go wrong at the last minute.

With only 300 miles to Arklow, fog descended at dusk and drove the wind off somewhere else. A thick silent cloud lay on deck making it impossible to see further than the bow. Keeping a visual watch throughout the night was impossible. They resorted to listening for the sound of approaching ships and calling on the VHF every half hour to anyone who might be within radio range. After two hours of this acoustic watch it was difficult not to waken to the slightest alteration in the gentle noise of *Poitín*'s roll. He lay staring into the blackness of the cabin while Tina listened intently to the rhythm of the night. A call came through on the VHF, 'Small craft, possibly a yacht, position 46°47'North, 15°38' West ...' Tina answered the call in the offchance it might be for *Poitín* and was greeted by the captain of a German ship who had noticed a tiny dot on his radar. He first passed on the position of other ships in the area followed by a detailed weather forecast for the next 24 hours.

With the rising sun came a gentle breeze which carried the fog off to an unknown place. By Saturday they were only 350 miles from Arklow. *Poitín* romped along in perfect conditions and he estimated they would arrive some time on Tuesday. A bottle of Portuguese port was opened after the evening meal to toast *Poitín*'s safety but his preoccupation with the last few hundred miles prevented him from visualising her safe return. He remembered the Australian woman who sailed around the world single-handed only to finish on the rocks off Sydney. 'Anything could happen,' he thought.

The prospect of reaching Ireland after such an eventful trip had them bursting with excitement. To add to the sense of homecoming they picked up Irish radio broadcasting a concert 'live from Dublin'. He cast his mind back to when he had listened to the same station fade as *Poitín* carried him south from Ireland. He remembered the anxiety and apprehension at what he imagined lay ahead and how he had wondered if he would make it across the Atlantic alone. Now he was returning, having experienced more than he had ever imagined and all that was required was to keep a cool head and get *Poitín* safely home. 'Anything can happen,' he repeated.

***

It was late Monday afternoon when he sighted Ireland and called to Tina at the top of his voice. She rushed up on deck to see a faint shadow on the horizon like an aura above the land. They danced with delight, round and round, their bodies swaying, their feet shuffling in the confines of the cockpit floor and as they danced their hearts celebrated with cheers and laughter that filled the emptiness of the ocean. Tina had never been to Ireland.

The sky was near to empty except for the cloud silt left by the ebbing day. They sat on deck immersed in the magnificence of the scene. In the background a strong Irish accent gave a favourable weather forecast on the VHF radio. The voice then said 'Radio traffic for Yacht *Poitín*'. They were confused by the message and wondered if there might be another *Poitín* in the area. He doubted the VHF could transmit as far as the land-based station but tried anyway, 'Rosslare Radio, Rosslare Radio, Rosslare Radio, this is Yacht *Poitín* over'. They waited a moment and to their surprise received a reply asking if they would accept a call from Wales. Tina's dad had watched the weather for the past ten days and calculated that *Poitín* would be off Rosslare by the end of the month. She was ecstatic at hearing her parents' voices and spoke excitedly of seeing them again. He left the cabin and the intimacy of her family conversation and from the bow he prayed for *Poitín*'s safe return.

Poitín trickled through the night barely holding her own against the tide and it was early morning before Tuskar Rock lighthouse was rounded. She crawled through the day, ticking off distant headlands on the East Coast chart. He considered sailing through the banks in order to work the tides but a whisper warned him to stay well clear. Late on Tuesday afternoon *Poitín* eventually arrived in Arklow Bay and they set about preparing to enter port. All the courtesy flags from the countries visited since leaving Arklow were hoisted and the deck tidied. The excitement of the long-awaited arrival was now tempered with a sense of calm and achievement. They were ecstatic at the prospect of arriving safely but knew they owed special thanks for being allowed to pass. Conversation was punctuated with long silences in which they considered their thoughts.

He left Tina in the cockpit and sat with his diary on the fore-deck. The Wicklow Mountains rose high into the evening sky while Arklow waited by the shore. Nothing appeared to have changed. He observed *Poitín*'s return, remembered her departure and for a brief moment there was nothing in between. An ocean full of events, of people and conversations, flooded into his mind. Nothing would ever be the same. He opened his diary and wrote:

Arklow, aprox. four miles off.

'A humbling experience' is how I would describe the past year. Sure, there were times in port when I got drunk and acted the idiot, but there were also special moments at sea when I was alone with my Creator. Never before have I encountered such power and love emanating from one source. As a living being I felt God could have crushed me at any second without even noticing but as a loving soul I was of the utmost importance.

For years, I tried to imagine what ocean sailing had to offer in my quest to find peace of mind. I knew there was the possibility of becoming more spiritually aware but what I did not expect was to return to my childhood and see myself as an innocent soul who had yet to be hardened by the world and all its fears. It is frightening to see the changes that have occurred in me. Many of those changes are based on fear and only act to inhibit my life rather than enhance it in any way. They involve erecting barriers around my heart and emotions in order to adjust to adulthood. I now know that no matter how much I protect myself, the pure and loving soul that first arrived on this Earth is still deep inside me. No longer do I look at the hardened adult and believe that is all there is to me. My hope for the future is that the adult can continue to learn from the free and innocent child.

There is no doubt in my mind now that unknown to our conscious minds we choose our path in life. Why some people suffer more than others seems cruel and unjust but maybe that is how a soul finds the experiences it requires to fulfil its purpose in this life.

I know that I would have made a dreadful mistake if I had not heeded my heart. If anyone were to ask me should they take a chance, should they strive to fulfil a dream, I would say yes, as long as it is within their reach. Too many people have destroyed themselves pursuing someone else's expectations. As long as we are true to ourselves and give our best, then we can achieve something in our lifetime. The real prize lies in the lessons learnt during the struggle.

It's a weird but wonderful world and it holds an Aladdin's Cave of experiences to enjoy. We all have a need to express ourselves and we all have a soul that wants to be heard. Some people write books, some paint pictures, and others sail boats across oceans. *Poitín* is the brush with which I painted my soul upon the sea.

A flotilla of boats from the sailing club greeted *Poitín* as she approached the harbour entrance. The local Lifeboat joined them and sprayed water into the air. Yachts blew their horns and people cheered as *Poitín* made her way across the harbour to the Sailing Club jetty. The quayside was lined with those who had read in the local paper of *Poitín's* Atlantic voyage. Dermot had not set any records, other than a personal best, but that was enough for friends and neighbours to offer a hero's welcome. He felt moved when he saw the few remaining schooner sailors applaud from the quayside.

Tina and he stood with big silly grins on their faces and felt a bond they knew no one else could understand. The intense experiences of the 4,000-mile voyage had brought them closer together than decades of polite friendship. The humility which the ocean extracted as its price for letting them pass left little room for pretence. They had seen each other react to the prospect of dying in a cold and alien environment. They had witnessed the childish euphoria that erupted as their emotional pendulum swung from bad days to good. Most importantly they had shared moments of weakness. For years he had refused to be dependent on any woman because he feared revealing his vulnerability but like all fears, once confronted, it would become a strength.

In the midst of all the fun and excitement it seemed there was someone missing and he remembered *Poitín*, steady and determined, carrying him home. To see her back in Arklow filled him with pride. How could she begin to tell the other boats where she had been? How could she describe what she had endured to see him through the worst?

Poitín nudged against the jetty, her fenders rolling as she drew to a final halt. Hands grabbed her and hands held her safely and hands reached for lines to tie her to the shore. Dermot's parents waited anxiously, waiting for the moment they had sometimes feared might never come. He jumped ashore and hugged his mother. Lifting her off her feet he kissed her and blabbered words he hoped would touch the delight he felt at seeing her again. She too struggled for words. 'Oh Dermot, thank God you are safe,' she said. 'You're home, you're safe ... I love you Dermot.' She began to cry and then laughed for crying when her heart brimmed with joy. They both smiled and she pleaded to be put down before he broke her old arthritic bones. 'I love you too, Mum,' he said, resting her gently on her twisted feet.

Over her shoulder he saw his Dad's face big with smiling and eyes almost full. There stood his childhood hero waiting to embrace him and say, as best he knew how, that he was 'a good little boy.' But first he commented that *Poitín* was not properly secured to the shore. Dermot smiled and thought how glad he was his hero still cared. No longer was there the need for a sharp reply because before him stood a man who beamed with love, a love his son could now see. They hugged and patted each other on the back, gibbering words of greeting and affection. 'Dermot, it's great to see you home safely. God I was so afraid ...'

'Don't, Dad. it's OK, I'm home now,' he whispered, pulling him closer. 'It's great to see you again. I love you dearly Dad.'

'Yes, of course, yes, I missed you too,' he said hoping his son would understand. He felt his father tremble, thought he heard a generation cry and held him as though he were *his* son.

OTHER TITLES FROM THIS PRESS

BLACK CAT IN THE WINDOW
Liam Ó Murchú
1-898256-85-3   £8.99 PB

This vivid memoir opens on a tenement floor and largely stays there as the author traces his childhood in days of incredible poverty, when wealth meant having good neighbours and hygiene having no rats. A tale of human endurance and much love.

'... flows with lyrical prose ... crackling abundance of colourful characters.'
Irish Independent

THE KEEPER OF ABSALOM'S ISLAND
Tom Nestor
1-898256-82-9   £8.99 PB

This account of growing up in rural Ireland in the 1940s describes a vanished way of life and the simplicity and beauty of that time and place. It also deals with the young boy's limited horizons, emerging conflicts with religion and convention, the futile endeavour to reach his father and the many colourful characters that inform Tom's childhood.

'Huckleberry Finn crossed with Tarry Flynn.'
Sunday Tribune

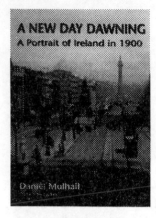

A New Day Dawning
A Portrait of Ireland in 1900
Dan Mulhall
1-898256-65-9   £20.00 HB

Focused primarily on the year 1900, this book describes politics, economic circumstances, literary and cultural achievements and way of life. The final chapters describe the world outside, putting Ireland in an international context and the book concludes with comparisons and contrasts between Ireland in 1900 and Ireland at the turn of the new millennium.

'... an enthralling account ... deserves a wide and relfective readership.'
J.J. Lee

Stop! – Break Free from the Tyranny of the Urgent
Barry McCullough
1-898256-43-8   £8.99 PB

Written as a novel, *Stop!* contains specific techniques to help you on your voyage of self-discovery. The book gives you powerful strategies that you can implement right now to reclaim the kind of life you always wanted but never thought possible.

The book centres on Cormac, a successful management consultant, and his daughter Fiona, locked in a mid-career trap. Based on his holistic approach to work and living, Cormac helps her cope with the challenge of change as she builds a better way of life.

SONGS FROM THE WOMB
HEALING THE WOUNDED MOTHER
Benig Mauger
1-898256-54-3   £9.99 PB

In a groundbreaking book, Benig Mauger places birth and life in the womb as a formative soul experience creating patterns we carry with us into later life. Based on her experiences as a birth teacher, therapist and mother, Benig writes about the joys and the pains of giving birth.

'This is simply a stunning book'
                    Sunday Independent

INTIMACY
THE NOBLE ADVENTURE
Don and Martha Rosenthal
1-898256-77-2   £7.99 PB

This book presents a vision of intimacy as a path to self-knowledge and love, without spiritual clichés or psychological jargon. It addresses the difficulty of intimacy in a most practical manner, showing couples how to go through confusion, resentment, guilt, fear, pain, etc., yet emerge richer for having undergone these difficulties.

'I keep this book beside my bed at all times'
                    Stephen Pearse

REIKI AT HAND
Teresa Collins
1-898256-40-3   £12.99 PB

Reiki, meaning 'life energy', is an ancient healing system using the universal life energy to heal. It works at both a physical and an emotional level. Teresa Collins qualified for Reiki in 1984 and is now a 'Master Level' instructor. This is the first instruction book to cover all three levels of Reiki, with step-by-step instructions and workshop programmes. It includes guidelines and contra indications for using Reiki and discusses its history and philosophy.

'answers many important questions'
Reviewers Bookwatch

CELTIC RITUALS
Alexei Kondratiev
1-898256-91-8   £6.99 PB

Certain cultures in various parts of the world have maintained a respectful and balanced relationship with their natural environment. Many people today are turning to them to learn how to rediscover these ancient and sacred attitudes. This book shows you how to become conversant with Celtic culture and mythology. The book provides an actual formula of words for each of the Celtic rituals and visualisation sequences.

'A book by a very learned man, for a New Age'
Prof. Daithí Ó hOgáin